Studio

D1627945

AQA GCSE French
Grammar & Translation Workbook

Stuart Glover

ALWAYS LEARNING

PEARSON

How to use your Grammar and Translation Workbook

This workbook is divided into 3 sections:

1 Grammar and translation

This section provides lots of useful practice and support as you work through *Studio AQA GCSE French*. Master key grammar points with the help of clear explanations and examples followed by focussed grammar and translation exercises.

Look out for links to pages in your *Studio AQA GCSE French* Higher or Foundation Student Book, for more on a particular grammar point:

» *Foundation: pp. 10–11*
» *Higher: pp. 8–9*

(Note: the grammar points in this workbook aren't just linked to the topics where you first encounter them in the Student Book, though – they cover a wider range of vocabulary to give you the confidence to be able to understand and use grammar in lots of different contexts.)

Exercises and explanations marked with the symbol **Ⓗ** are aimed at users of the Higher Student Book. Why not give them a try?

2 Translation in practice

Brush up on useful strategies to help you tackle translations before putting into practice all of the grammar, vocabulary and translation skills you have learned, with this bank of translation activities covering all of the different topics you will need to know for your exams. This is a great way to revise grammar and vocabulary at the end of your course (and you'll need to tackle translation questions in your AQA GCSE Reading and Writing exams, so this is great practice!)

3 Verb tables

A handy list of regular and irregular verbs in the key tenses you'll need to know, to refer to whenever you need!

Tips

Look out for the following tips to help you as you work through the book:

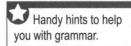 Handy hints to help you with grammar.

Clues to help you translate a specific word or phrase.

 Useful strategies to remember for your translations.

Answers

Answers to all of the exercises and model translations for every translation task are available on our online *ActiveLearn Digital Service* – just ask your teacher who will have access to these.

Published by Pearson Education Limited, 80 Strand, London, WC2R 0RL.

www.pearsonschoolsandfecolleges.co.uk

Text © Pearson Education Limited 2016
Edited by Melissa Weir
Designed by Tek-Art, East Grinstead, West Sussex
Typeset by Tek-Art, East Grinstead, West Sussex
Produced by Cambridge Publishing Management
Original illustrations © Pearson Education Limited 2016
Illustrated by Tek-Art, Beehive Illustration, KJA Artists and John Hallett.
Cover photo © Alamy/kevers

First published 2016

19 18 17 16
10 9 8 7 6 5 4 3 2 1

British Library Cataloguing in Publication Data
A catalogue record for this book is available from the British Library

ISBN 978 1 292 13288 4

Copyright notice
All rights reserved. No part of this publication may be reproduced in any form or by any means (including photocopying or storing it in any medium by electronic means and whether or not transiently or incidentally to some other use of this publication) without the written permission of the copyright owner, except in accordance with the provisions of the Copyright, Designs and Patents Act 1988 or under the terms of a licence issued by the Copyright Licensing Agency, Saffron House, 6–10 Kirby Street, London EC1N 8TS (www.cla.co.uk). Applications for the copyright owner's written permission should be addressed to the publisher.

Printed in Italy by Lego S.p.A

Acknowledgements
We would like to thank Melanie Birdsall, Florence Bonneau, Charonne Prosser, Fabienne Tartarin and Melissa Weir for their invaluable help in the development of this book.

Contents

1. Grammar and translation

G Gender

Every French noun has a gender, either **masculine** (m) or **feminine** (f). All people, places or things are either masculine or feminine and it is easier to learn the French noun with its gender. You will need to know a noun's gender because every time you use an adjective with a noun, you might need to change its spelling if the noun is feminine or plural.

There are some clues which will help you remember the gender of a noun:

★ If you don't know the gender of a word, you can look it up in a dictionary or online.

Masculine nouns

• male people:	*le père*	father
• days of the week:	*le lundi*	on Mondays
• seasons:	*le printemps*	spring
• most nouns which end in *–age*:	*le vill**age***	village
• most nouns which end in *–er*:	*le bouch**er***	butcher
• most nouns which end in *–eau*:	*le bur**eau***	office __except__ *l'eau (f)* water

Feminine nouns

• female people:	*la mère*	mother
• countries which end in *–e*:	*la Franc**e***	France
• most nouns which end in *–e*:	*la voitur**e***	car
• most nouns which end in *–ée*:	*la journ**ée***	day
• all nouns ending in *–sion* or *–tion*:	*la destina**tion***	destination
• all nouns ending in *–té*:	*l'identi**té***	identity

Some nouns are __always feminine__, whether they are referring to a male or female person: *la vedette* (star), *la personne* (person), *la victime* (victim).

Some nouns are __always masculine__ such as *le bébé* (baby).

Many masculine nouns have a feminine equivalent which is formed by adding *–e*: e.g. *ami* → *amie* (friend). Others simply change gender depending on the person to whom the noun refers: e.g. *collègue* can be masculine or feminine.

Jobs often change their ending to make the feminine form:

le mécanicien (m) → *la mécanicienne (f)*   mechanic
le coiffeur (m) → *la coiffeuse (f)*   hairdresser
le boulanger (m) → *la boulangère (f)*   baker

★ Don't assume you know the gender of a word in French just because you know what it means. For example, it's **la police** (f)!

Some nouns change meaning depending on their gender:

le tour (m)   tour / trick   **but**   *la tour (f)*   tower

Plural nouns

To make a French noun plural, you normally add *–s*: *chat* → *chats* (but the *–s* is not pronounced!).

Some nouns end in *–x* in the plural:

- nouns ending in *–al*: *animal* → *animaux* (animal → animals)
- nouns ending in *–eau*: *bureau* → *bureaux* (office → offices)
- nouns ending in *–eu*: *jeu* → *jeux* (game → games)
- some nouns ending in *–ail*: *travail* → *travaux* (work → works)
- some nouns ending in *–ou*: *genou* → *genoux* (knee → knees).

H Nouns which already end in *–x*, *–z* or *–s* don't change: e.g. *os* (bone *or* bones), *nez* (nose *or* noses).

Abstract nouns, which are used to talk about qualities, are always singular:

la générosité (generosity), *la modestie* (modesty), *la fidélité* (faithfulness)

Studio GCSE French © Pearson Education Limited 2016

1 **Work out the gender of these words. Write m (masculine) or f (feminine).**

1 fille _f_ 2 garage _f_ 3 plage _f_ 4 hiver _m_ 5 quantité _f_
6 oncle _m_ 7 décision _m_ 8 bébé _f_ 9 araignée _f_ 10 père _m_

2 **Make the following nouns plural.**

1 chou _✗_ 2 hôtel _s_ 3 riz _____ 4 chien _s_ 5 travail _aux_

3 **Fill in the gaps in the table.**

	singular	plural
1	Chat	chats
2	animal	animaux
3	château	châteaux
4	fils	fils
5	nez	nez

4 **Write the French job titles.**

1 _____ 2 un médecin 3 _____ 4 un professeur

5 une fermièr 6 une femme d'affaire 7 un fermier 8 vendeuse

5 **Now fill in the gaps with the correct word.**

⭐ You may need to use a dictionary to help you here!

masculine	feminine	English meaning
caissier	caissière	cashier
électricien	électricienne	electrician
fermièr	fermière	farmer
fonctionnaire	fonctionnaire	civil servant
journalist	journaliste	journalist
vendeur	vendeuse	sales assistant
vétérinaire	vétérinaire	vet

Ⓖ Definite articles

As you know, every French noun is either masculine or feminine. The French for 'the' is different for masculine and feminine nouns. *Le* is used before masculine nouns and *la* before feminine: e.g. *le livre* (the book), *la table* (the table). *Les* is used for all plural nouns whatever their gender: e.g. *les livres* (the books), *les tables* (the tables).

However, *le* and *la* both change to *l'* if the noun is singular and starts with a vowel or silent *h*. In these cases, you cannot tell by looking whether the noun is masculine or feminine, so it is very important to learn the genders of nouns: e.g. *l'église* (f) the church <u>but</u> *l'hôpital* (m) the hospital.

	masculine	feminine	before a vowel or silent *h*	plural
The definite article: 'the'	le	la	l'	les

Indefinite articles

The French for 'a' is either *un* (for masculine words) or *une* (for feminine words): e.g. *un livre* (a book), *une table* (a table). The plural of the indefinite article is *des* (some): e.g. *des livres* (some books), *des tables* (some tables).

	masculine	feminine	plural
The indefinite article: 'a' or 'some' (pl)	un	une	des

1 Write the correct word for 'the' (*le, la, l'* or *les*) in front of these places in a town.

1 *la* pharmacie (f)

2 *le* hôtel (m)

3 *la* gare (f)

4 *les* magasins (pl)

5 *le* bowling (m)

6 *le* cinéma (m)

7 *le* hôpital (m)

8 *les* appartements (pl)

9 *les* rues (pl)

10 *la* piscine (f)

2 Write the correct word for 'a' (*un* or *une*) in front of the following parts of the house.

1 *un* jardin

2 *une* salle de bains

3 *un* salon

4 *une* cuisine

5 *une* chambre

6 *une* salle à manger

7 *une* garage

8 *une* salle de séjour

3 Fill in the gaps in this table.

singular	plural
le livre	les livres
un magasin	les magasins
l'hôtel	les hôtels
de maison	des maisons
l'arbre	les arbres
un parking	un parking
de plage	des plages
une piscine	les piscines

⭐ Look carefully at the articles (*un, une, des, le, la, l', les*).

Studio GCSE French © Pearson Education Limited 2016

4 Translate the following into French.

1 the streets   les rues ✓

2 some trees   des ~~les~~ arbres ✓

3 a swimming pool   une piscine ✓

4 a church   une église ✓

5 some cinemas   des cinémas ✓

6 the hospital   l'hôpital ✓

7 a car park   un parking ✓

8 some markets   des marchés ✓

9 the park   le parc ✓

10 the shops   les magasins ✓

> ⭐ If there is a feminine word starting with a vowel or silent *h*, the French is still *une*: **une église** a church.

5 Translate these sentences into French.

1 I like the cinema.

J'aime le cinéma ✓

2 I don't like books.

Je n'aime pas les livres ✓

> Remember that there must be a word for 'the' in French here.

3 I prefer the theatre.

Je préfère le théâtre ✓

Ⓗ 6 Translate this passage into French.

> Remember: 'a' is an indefinite article.

> 'Some' is also an indefinite article.

> 'The' is a definite article.

In my town there is a shopping centre with some fantastic shops. I like the bowling alley but I don't like the museum. There are also some cafés, some restaurants and an ice rink. The railway station is opposite the swimming pool and the beach is behind the railway station.

Dans ma ville il y a un centre commercial avec des magasins fantastique. J'aime le bowling mais je n'aime pas le musée. Il y a aussi des cafés, des restaurants et une patinoire. la gare est en face de la piscine et la plage est derrière la gare.

Articles The partitive article

>> Foundation pp .50–51
>> Higher pp. 52–53

G It is important to know when and how to use the partitive article, as it translates the English word 'some'. The word you use will depend on whether the noun is masculine, feminine or plural, and whether it begins with a vowel or silent 'h'.

masculine	feminine	begins with vowel or silent 'h'	plural
du	de la	de l'	des

du café some coffee   *de l'eau* some water
de la confiture some jam   *des chips* some crisps

We don't always need to say 'some' in English, but it must be used in French.

Tu veux du sucre?   Do you want (some) sugar?

However, after a negative, you must use *de* (or *d'* before a vowel or a silent 'h'). In such cases, we would say 'any' rather than 'some' in English.

Nous n'avons pas de lait.   We don't have **any** milk.

You must use the word for 'some' in questions, although we would use 'any' in English.

Vous avez du pain?   Have you got **any** bread?

Similarly, expressions of quantity are followed by *de* or *d'* too.

une bouteille d'eau   a bottle **of** water   or *un paquet de chips*   a packet **of** crisps

1 Write the correct word for 'some' in front of these nouns.

1 _____ bonbons (pl)   5 _____ pain (m)

2 _____ jambon (m)   6 _____ frites (pl)

3 _____ petits pois (pl)   7 _____ huile (f)

4 _____ viande (f)   8 _____ confiture (f)

2 Complete the sentences with *du/de la/de l'* or *des*.

1 Tu as _____ légumes?   3 J'ai _____ eau minérale.   5 Nous avons _____ carottes.

2 Tu voudrais _____ café?   4 Tu voudrais _____ pizza?

3 You need to go shopping. Write answers to these questions, saying whether you have the following things.

⭐ Remember that you always use *de* (or *d'*) after a negative.

Example: Tu as des pêches? Non, je n'ai pas de pêches.

1 Tu as du pain? ✗

_____

2 Vous avez des pommes? ✓

_____

3 Tu as de l'eau minérale? ✓

_____

4 Tu as de la viande? ✗

_____

5 Vous avez du fromage? ✓

_____

4 **Translate these sentences into English.**

1 Nous n'avons pas de garage.

....

2 Elle n'a pas de frères.

....

3 Tu as des livres.

....

4 Ont-ils de l'argent?

....

5 Je n'ai pas de chips.

....

5 **Translate these sentences into French.**

1 I don't have any brothers.

....

> Remember that after a negative you must use *de* (or *d'*).

2 I would like some coffee.

....

> This word will depend on the gender of the noun.

3 I want some eggs, some ham, some jam and some mineral water.

....

4 Do you want some coffee?

....

5 Would you like some bananas?

....

6 Do you have you any money?

....

H 6 **Translate this passage into French.**

> Think about the tense here!

I want some milk, some butter and some flour because I am going to make a cake. I bought some peaches and some pears yesterday. I have lots of fruit but I would also like some apples and some cream. I haven't got any sugar but I have got some yoghurt. Do you have any eggs?

> After a negative, 'any' is often *de*.

....

....

....

....

Adjectives Agreement and position

» *Foundation pp. 6–7*
» *Higher pp. 6–7, p. 54*

 Adjectives are words that describe people or things, so they are very important when you want to develop greater range or complexity in what you write or say in French. When you use adjectives, you must think about <u>agreement</u> and <u>position</u>.

Regular adjectives

Adjectives must agree with the noun they describe.
Regular adjectives ending in a consonant add an **–e** for feminine, **–s** for masculine plural and **–es** for feminine plural:

masculine singular	feminine singular	masculine plural	feminine plural
grand	grand**e**	grand**s**	grand**es**
petit	petit**e**	petit**s**	petit**es**

Some adjectives already end in **–e** so don't add another:

timide	timide	timid**es**	timid**es**

Similarly, if an adjective ends in **–s**, you don't add another in the masculine plural:

gris	gris**e**	gris	gris**es**

Sometimes, this changes how the adjective is pronounced: e.g. *vert/verte, brun/brune*.

Irregular adjectives do not follow the rules. As many of these are common adjectives, they are very important and need to be learned.

- Adjectives ending in **–x**, change to **–se** in the feminine: *dangereux* ➜ *dangereuse*.
- Adjectives ending in **–f**, change to **–ve** in the feminine: *sportif* ➜ *sportive*.
- Adjectives ending in **–er**, change to **–ère** in the feminine: *dernier* ➜ *dernière*.
- Adjectives ending in **–on**, **–en** or **–il** double the consonant before adding **–e** in the feminine: *mignon* ➜ *mignonne*, *canadien* ➜ *canadienne* and *gentil* ➜ *gentille*.

Some adjectives don't follow a fixed rule:

masculine singular	feminine singular	masculine plural	feminine plural
long	long**ue**	long**s**	long**ues**
blanc	blan**che**	blancs	blan**ches**
gros	gros**se**	gros	gros**ses**
sec	s**èche**	secs	s**èches**
vieux	vie**ille**	vieux	vie**illes**

Some adjectives such as *marron* (brown) and *orange* (orange) never change: *une écharpe **marron*** (a brown scarf)

Using **clair** (light) and **foncé** (dark) with colours makes the colour invariable (it stays in the masculine singular form): *une chemise **bleu clair*** (a light blue shirt), ***des** chaussettes **vert foncé*** (dark green socks).

Position of adjectives

Most adjectives (including all colours) come <u>after</u> the noun they describe: e.g. *les yeux **bleus*** (blue eyes) or *une histoire **intéressante*** (an interesting story).

However, a few common adjectives come <u>before</u> the noun:

*une **petite** maison*   a small house   *un **joli** jardin*   a pretty garden

grand(e)	big	*vieux/vieille*	old	*jeune*	young	*haut(e)*	high / tall
petit(e)	small	*nouveau/nouvelle*	new	*bon/bonne*	good	*meilleur(e)*	best
joli(e)	pretty	*beau/belle*	beautiful	*mauvais(e)*	bad		

1 **Write the correct form of the adjective in brackets.**

⭐ Remember that you may need to change the spelling of the adjective to make it agree with the noun it describes.

1 Le chien est _____ (*noir*).

2 Nous avons une _____ (*grand*) maison.

3 Elle a les yeux _____ (*vert*).

4 Ma _____ (*petit*) sœur m'énerve.

5 Mes sœurs sont _____ (*bavard*).

6 Ma tante est _____ (*aimable*).

Studio GCSE French © Pearson Education Limited 2016

2 **Complete this table with the correct form of the adjectives.**

masculine singular	feminine singular	masculine plural	feminine plural	English meaning
bleu	bleue			blue
sérieux		sérieux		
	active			active
gentil				kind
blanc		blancs		

3 **Using the correct form of the adjectives in the box below, complete the sentences.**

1 Les crayons sont _____ (*white*).

2 Elle a trois _____ (*little*) sœurs.

3 Ma tante est _____ (*kind*).

4 Ma sœur est _____ (*cute*).

5 Mon frère est très _____ (*optimistic*).

6 J'ai une _____ (*new*) chambre.

nouveau
mignon
petit
blanc
gentil
optimiste

⭐ Don't forget to change the adjective's spelling if it needs to agree.

4 **Put the adjectives in brackets in the correct place in the sentence and make them agree if necessary.**

1 Mon ami est triste. (*meilleur*) _____

2 Elle a les cheveux. (*court*) _____

3 Il y a un parc près de chez moi. (*joli*) _____

4 J'ai des copains. (*travailleur*) _____

5 J'ai une amie. (*égoïste*) _____

5 **Translate these sentences into French.**

1 The little girl is very chatty.

_____

Remember that 'girl' is feminine.

2 She has long hair and brown eyes.

_____

Remember that *marron* never changes.

3 The boys are kind but serious.

_____

Remember that 'boys' is plural.

ⓗ 6 **Translate this description of your friends into French.**

Think about the position of the adjectives.

Ellie: She is very tall and slim and she has black hair and green eyes. She is chatty and cute.

Polly: She is quite small and she has long brown hair and grey eyes. She is shy but kind.

Marc: He is tall and fat and has short blond hair and blue eyes. He has a big nose.

Remember where 'big' comes in the sentence.

_____

_____

_____

_____

_____

_____

Adjectives Possessive adjectives

» *Foundation p. 6, pp. 12–13*
» *Higher p. 12*

Ⓖ Possessive adjectives are used to say 'my', 'your', 'our', their', etc., so they are very useful. They work in the same way as other adjectives; they change according to gender and number. There are usually three different words, depending on whether the noun they describe is masculine, feminine or plural.

English meaning	masculine	feminine	plural
my	mon	ma	mes
your (familiar)	ton	ta	tes
his/her/its	son	sa	ses
our	notre	notre	nos
your (polite/plural)	votre	votre	vos
their	leur	leur	leurs

mon frère (my brother), *ma* sœur (my sister), *mes* parents (my parents)

It is really important to remember that the possessive adjectives agree with the noun they describe, not with the person that the noun belongs to: e.g. *son frère* means 'her' brother, as 'brother' is masculine; *sa sœur* means 'his' sister,' as 'sister' is feminine.

Note that there are only two forms for *notre/nos*, *votre/vos* and *leur/leurs*, as the masculine and feminine forms are identical.

You need to be careful when there is a feminine noun which starts with a vowel or silent *h*, as in these cases you must use *mon*, *ton* or *son*, not *ma*, *ta* or *sa*: e.g. *ton amie*   your (female) friend.

1 Add *mon, ma* or *mes* to these nouns.

1 _____ père

2 _____ mère

3 _____ grand-père

4 _____ sœurs

5 _____ oncle

6 _____ famille

7 _____ parents

8 _____ tante

2 Choose the correct possessive adjective to complete these sentences.

1 *Mon / Ma / Mes* frères sont intelligents.

2 *Notre / Nos* collège est grand.

3 *Leur / Leurs* cahiers sont bleus.

4 *Ton / Ta / Tes* village est petit.

5 *Son / Sa / Ses* ville est industrielle.

6 *Votre / Vos* professeur est sévère.

3 Complete the sentences with the correct French word for the word in brackets.

1 J'aime _____ (*her*) collège.

2 Je n'aime pas _____ (*our*) professeurs.

3 Je déteste _____ (*their*) copain.

4 Je m'entends bien avec _____ (*my*) amie, Sylvie.

5 J'adore _____ (*his*) chiens.

6 Elle aime _____ (*your*, tu *part*) maison.

7 Ils s'entendent avec _____ (*your*, tu *part*) parents.

8 Nous admirons _____ (*your*, vous *part*) robe.

Studio GCSE French © Pearson Education Limited 2016

4 Fill in the gaps with the correct possessive adjective: *son*, *sa* or *ses*.

Alice s'occupe de **1** _____ famille. Elle travaille comme dentiste et **2** _____ mari est professeur.

Elle s'entend bien avec **3** _____ deux enfants. Louise, **4** _____ fille, a douze ans et Matthieu,

5 _____ fils, a dix ans.

5 Translate these sentences into English.

1 Mon père et ma mère sont contents.

_____

2 Son anniversaire est en avril.

_____

> Remember that *son* could be translated in two ways here.

3 Dans leur village il n'y a pas de magasins.

_____

4 Tes parents sont gentils.

_____

_____

6 Translate these sentences into French.

> The two words for 'her' in this sentence will be different.

1 Her house isn't very comfortable but her garden is big.

_____

2 My friends are quite shy and very hard-working.

_____

3 Their school is well equipped.

_____

H 7 Translate this passage into French.

Our house is small but our living room is great. I like my room because it is quite big. My door is blue and my curtains are pink. My friend Annette lives nearby. Her flat is spacious and her bedroom is enormous but there is no garden.

> You can translate 'nearby' as *tout près*.

> 'Her' will depend on the gender of 'flat' and 'bedroom'.

_____

_____

_____

_____

_____

Studio GCSE French © Pearson Education Limited 2016

Adjectives Comparative adjectives

» *Foundation p. 39*
» *Higher pp. 36–37*

G You use the comparative when you are comparing two things. In French it is easy to do this as you simply put ***plus*** 'more' or ***moins*** 'less' in front of the adjective. The adjectives still have to agree with the nouns they describe.

*Mon frère est grand. Mon ami Paul est **plus** grand.*	My brother is tall. My friend Paul is tall**er** (more tall).
*Ma sœur est petite. Mon amie Lucy est **plus** petite.*	My sister is small. My friend Lucy is small**er** (more small).
*Mon oncle est intelligent. Mon frère est **moins** intelligent.*	My uncle is intelligent. My brother is **less** intelligent.

When you want to compare two things in one sentence you need to use ***plus/moins*** + **adjective** followed by ***que***.

*Paul est **plus** grand **que** Simon.*
Paul is tall**er** **than** Simon.

Paul   Simon

*Lucy est **plus** petite **que** Sophie.*
Lucy is small**er** **than** Sophie.

Sophie Lucy

If you want to say that something or someone is <u>as</u> big / tall / intelligent <u>as</u> something or someone, use ***aussi*** + **adjective** followed by ***que***.

*Mon collège est **aussi** grand **que** ton collège.*
My school is **as** big **as** your school.

1 Choose the correct comparative.

1 Marc est *plus petit / plus petite* que Samir.

2 Marianne est *plus grand / plus grande* que Janine.

3 Mes copains sont *plus gentils / plus gentil* que tes copains.

4 Le dessin est *plus intéressant / plus intéressante* que l'anglais.

5 La chimie est *plus barbant / plus barbante* que la physique.

> ⭐ Remember that the adjective will agree with the <u>first</u> thing being compared.

2 Write these sentences in the correct order.

Example: ma plus grande maison maison ta est que   *Ma maison est plus grande que ta maison.*

1 la que plus musique est le français intéressant ....

2 ma frère grande est mon sœur moins que ....

3 mon aussi que intelligent père mère est ma ....

> ⭐ Remember that you will need to use *plus … que* in every sentence.

3 Translate these sentences into French.

1 She is more active than my sister. ....

> Remember that 'she' is feminine, so the adjective used must be feminine too.

2 French is easier than science. ....

3 Apples are more delicious than strawberries. ....

> Remember that 'apples' are feminine plural in French.

Studio GCSE French © Pearson Education Limited 2016

G You use the superlative when you are comparing more than two things. To form the superlative, add the definite article *le/la/les* and *plus* or *moins*.

le plus grand/*la plus* grande/*les plus* grand(e)s   the biggest

*Mon ami Alain est modeste. Mon copain Mohammed est plus modeste, mais mon ami Luc est **le plus** modeste.*
My friend Alain is modest. My mate Mohammed is more modest, but my friend Luc is **the most** modest.

However, you must be careful if you are describing a noun in this way, as the adjective takes its normal place (usually after the noun) and needs to agree.

*la matière **la moins** intéressante*   the **least** interesting subject

If an adjective normally comes <u>before</u> the noun, the superlative also comes first:

le plus grand problème   the bigg**est** problem

There are two important exceptions to the rule:

adjective	comparative	superlative	English meaning
bon	meilleur(e)	le meilleur/la meilleure	good → better → best
mauvais(e)	pire	le/la pire	bad → worse → the worst

H

*le **meilleur** professeur*
the **best** teacher

1 Use the adjective given in brackets, together with *le/la/les plus* or *le/la/les moins*, to make a superlative.

Example: Le sport est la matière (+ *intéressant*).   *Le sport est la matière la plus intéressante.*

1 L'été est la saison (+ *chaud*). _____

2 Londres est (+ *grand*) ville d'Angleterre. _____

3 Notre-Dame est la cathédrale (+ *important*). _____

4 Voilà les filles (– *sérieux*). _____

5 J'habite dans la ville (– *joli*). _____

6 Où est l'étudiant (– *intelligent*)? _____

2 Translate these sentences into French.

1 Fabien is the kindest. _____

2 Mount Everest is the highest mountain in the world. _____

3 Spanish is the best subject. _____

> 'Best' is an irregular superlative.

H 3 Now translate this passage into French.

> Where will 'hard' come in the sentence in French?

I think that art is the best subject at school. I don't like French because it is the hardest subject. History is more boring than geography but English is more interesting than maths. PE is the most tiring subject.

> Remember that this is feminine in French.

_____

_____

_____

_____

Adjectives Interrogative adjectives

» *Foundation p. 56*
» *Higher p. 83*

G Interrogative adjectives are used to translate the English 'which?' when you ask 'which book?', for example.
Like most adjectives, interrogatives have to agree with the noun they describe:

masculine singular	feminine singular	masculine plural	feminine plural
quel	quelle	quels	quelles

Quel garçon?   **Which** boy?   **Quels** garçons? **Which** boys?
Quelle fille?   **Which** girl?   **Quelles** filles?   **Which** girls?

The adjective isn't always <u>next to</u> the noun it describes but it still needs to <u>agree</u> with it. In those cases, the word may be translated into English as 'what?' rather than 'which?':

Quelle *est la date de ton anniversaire?*   **What** date is your birthday?
Quel *est le problème?*   **What** is the problem?

1 Choose the correct adjective to complete each sentence.

1 *Quel / Quelle* ville préfères-tu?

4 Tu aimes *quels / quelles* professeurs?

2 Tu aimes *quel / quelle* sandwich?

5 Vous aimez *quel / quelle* maison?

3 *Quels / Quelles* écharpes préférez-vous?

6 Tu préfères *quel / quelle* chien?

2 Complete the sentences with the correct word for 'which'.

1 C'est _____ jour?

2 Vous voulez _____ chaussures?

3 Tu voudrais essayer _____ chemise?

4 _____ hommes sont arrivés?

5 _____ pull aimes-tu?

6 Vous préférez _____ matières au collège?

Studio GCSE French © Pearson Education Limited 2016

3 Match the sentence halves to create the correct questions.

1 Quel est le…   a sont admis?

2 Vous fermez…   b problème?

3 Quels animaux…   c les possibilités?

4 Quelles sont…   d saison?

5 C'est quelle…   e quels jours de la semaine?

6 Quel…   f hôtel as-tu préféré?

> ⭐ You won't always use the same word order when you translate.

4 Translate these questions into English.

1 Quelle voiture préfères-tu? _____

2 Tu voudrais loger dans quel camping? _____

3 Vous préférez quelles cartes postales? _____

4 Tu vas aller à quel restaurant? _____

> ⭐ Remember that in French you can make a question by adding a question mark to the end of a statement.

5 Translate these questions into French.

1 Which shops do you like? _____

2 In which hotel are you staying? _____

3 Which visit did you prefer? _____

> Remember the gender of *visite*.

🔵 6 Translate this passage into French.

> Remember the gender of *heure*.

I don't know which film I'd like to watch or which cinema to go to. At what time does the cartoon start? After the film, which restaurants are open? Which bus can you catch to get home? Which shoes am I going to wear?

> Don't forget you can make a question just by adding a question mark to the end of a sentence.

> This is masculine plural.

> The French word order is the same. How will you translate 'you'?

> This is feminine plural.

_____
_____
_____
_____
_____

Adjectives Demonstrative adjectives

≫ *Foundation p. 57*
≫ *Higher p. 108*

G Demonstrative adjectives are 'this', 'that', 'these' and 'those', followed by a noun. You use them when you need to be precise about which person or thing you are talking about.

Like other adjectives, they need to <u>agree</u> with the word they describe.

	singular	plural
masculine	*ce livre* this book	*ces livres* these books
feminine	*cette table* this table	*ces tables* these tables

There is also a special form, **cet**, which is used in front of a **masculine singular** noun starting with a vowel or silent 'h'.

	cet hôtel	**this** hotel		*cet* étudiant	**this** student
but	*cette* idée	**this** idea (because *idée* is a feminine word)			

These adjectives can mean both 'this' or 'that' (singular) and 'these' or 'those' (plural). So, although it is sometimes obvious from the context which you mean, if you want to distinguish more clearly between 'this' and 'that', add '–*ci*' (for 'this') or '–*là*' (for 'that') to the end of the noun.

ce livre-ci	**this** book (here)	*ce livre-là*	**that** book (there)
ces tables-ci	**these** tables (here)	*ces tables-là*	**those** tables (there)

1 Write *ce, cet, cette* or *ces* in front of these nouns.

1 .... livre (m)   4 .... table (f)   7 .... homme (m)

2 .... robe (f)   5 .... église (f)   8 .... baskets (pl)

3 .... sandales (pl)   6 .... chaussures (pl)

⭐ Remember that you only use *cet* before a masculine singular noun which starts with a vowel or silent 'h'.

2 Match up the French and English phrases.

1 cette ceinture-ci   a this jumper

2 ces voitures-là   b that hotel

3 cet hôtel-là   c this belt

4 ces vélos-ci   d that jumper

5 ce pull-ci   e those cars

6 ce pull-là   f these bikes

⭐ Remember, –*ci* is added to emphasise 'this/these' and –*là* to emphasise 'that/those'.

3 Complete the sentences with the correct words in French.

1 J'aime .... (*this*) chien-ci.   4 Tu n'aimes pas .... (*those sweets*).

2 Elle préfère .... (*these shoes*).   5 Ils ont regardé .... (*this*) maison-ci.

3 Nous détestons .... (*that*) hôtel-là.   6 J'ai essayé .... (*that scarf*).

4 Translate these sentences into English.

1 Ces filles-là sont intelligentes. ....

2 Cette robe-ci est belle. ....

3 Je préfère ces baskets bleues. ....

5 Translate these sentences into French.

1 I like this dog. ....

2 I would like that shirt. ....

3 Do you like those cars? ....

Studio GCSE French © Pearson Education Limited 2016

Adjectives   Indefinite adjectives

G You use indefinite adjectives to talk about people or things in a general way, without being specific. There are a number of indefinite adjectives, but you just need to focus on **chaque** (each, every) and **quelque** (some, a few).

Chaque always describes a singular noun and you use the third person of the verb with it.
    Chaque *personne a essayé.*   **Each** person tried.

Quelque agrees with the word it describes, so adds an **–s** in the plural.
    pendant **quelque** *temps*   for **some** time
    Quelques *hommes sont arrivés.*   **Some/a few** men arrived.

1 Complete the sentences with the correct word in French.

1 _____ (*Every*) hôtel est très cher.

2 J'ai vu _____ (*some*) magasins.

3 _____ (*Some*) personnes sont là-bas.

4 J'ai fait ça _____ (*each*) fois.

5 _____ (*Every*) camping est bien équipé.

6 J'y suis resté pendant _____ (*some*) temps.

> *temps* is singular here.

2 Translate these sentences into English.

1 Je vais au collège à pied chaque matin.

_____

2 Il y a quelques cadeaux dans le salon.

_____

H 3 Je jouais au tennis chaque jour.

_____

H 4 J'y suis allé avec quelques copains.

_____

3 Translate these sentences into French.

1 I play football on Saturdays with some friends.

> No word for 'on' here.

_____

2 Every day I go into town.

> Remember that adjectives must agree with the word they describe.

_____

3 Some teachers are strict.

_____

H 4 Translate this passage into French.

> Look at p.18 to remind yourself which word you need here.

> Colours come after the word they describe in French.

> This is not one word in French.

> This is translated by a one-word verb in French.

I would like to buy those black shoes because they are fashionable. My friend prefers these grey sandals and my sister likes that red dress, but my brother hates this blue shirt. Every time that I look for clothes, there are a few problems.

_____

_____

_____

Quantifiers and intensifiers

» *Foundation p. 51*
» *Higher p. 53, p. 61*

G Quantifiers and intensifiers are used to add a little variety to your descriptions or to make them more precise. They are easy to use as they usually follow the same pattern as the English.

Quantifiers

Quantifiers are words which tell you <u>how much</u>. You can use them to give more precise amounts, so instead of saying something vague, like *des* (some), you could be more precise and say *beaucoup de* (lots of/a lot of) or even more exact, *un kilo de* (a kilo of).

Here are some important quantifiers:

assez de	enough of	*une boîte de*	a tin of
beaucoup de	a lot of	*une tranche de*	a slice of
une bouteille de	a bottle of	*un paquet de*	a packet of
une cannette de	a can of	*un morceau de*	a piece of
un kilo de	a kilo of	*un quart de*	a quarter of
un pot de	a pot of	*la moitié de*	half of
cinq cents grammes de	500g of	*un tiers de*	a third of
un litre de	a litre of		

*Je voudrais **une tranche de** ce gâteau s'il vous plait.*
*Il n'y a pas **assez de** magasins.*

I would like **a slice of** that cake please.
There aren't **enough** shops.

Intensifiers

Instead of merely describing someone or something as *grand*, you could add an intensifier to make the description more exact, or make the effect stronger:

*Il est **assez** grand.*   He's **quite** tall.   *Elle est **très** grande.*   She's **very** tall.

Here are some important intensifiers:

très	very	*un peu*	a little	*plutôt*	rather
assez	quite	*beaucoup*	much/many	*vraiment*	really
peu	little	*trop*	too	*énormément*	enormously

1 **Match up the correct English and French.**

1	Il est très petit.	**a**	She is quite tall.
2	Elle est assez petite.	**b**	They are really slim.
3	Ils sont trop timides.	**c**	He is very small.
4	Elles sont très bavardes.	**d**	She is quite small.
5	Elle est assez grande.	**e**	They are very chatty.
6	Ils sont vraiment minces.	**f**	They are too shy.

⭐ After an expression of quantity, *du*, *de la*, *de l'* and *des* all change to *de* (or *d'* before a vowel or silent *h*).

2 **Translate this shopping list into French.**

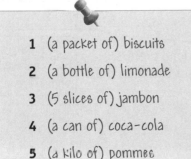

1	(a packet of) biscuits
2	(a bottle of) limonade
3	(5 slices of) jambon
4	(a can of) coca-cola
5	(a kilo of) pommes
6	(a piece of) pizza
7	(300g of) cheese

1 _____
2 _____
3 _____
4 _____
5 _____
6 _____
7 _____

Studio GCSE French © Pearson Education Limited 2016

3 Complete the text with the correct words in French.

Au collège, la journée scolaire est **1** _____ (*too long*)

et je suis **2** _____ (*quite tired*) après les cours. Je préfère le dessin car c'est

3 _____ (*very interesting*), mais je déteste l'anglais parce que c'est

4 _____ (*really boring*). J'ai **5** _____ (*lots of friends*)

et **6** _____ (*enough homework*).

> ⭐ Remember that any adjective must agree with the word it describes.

4 Translate these sentences into English.

1 Je voudrais un morceau de pizza.

_____

2 Ma copine est très généreuse.

_____

3 J'ai acheté beaucoup de livres.

_____

4 Elle aimerait un peu de sel.

_____

5 Translate these sentences into French.

1 I have lots of presents at Christmas.

_____

> Remember *beaucoup de…*

2 They are very happy.

_____

> Don't forget that 'happy' will need to agree with 'they'.

3 I would like to be quite rich.

_____

> 'Would like' is translated as one word in French.

🄷 6 Translate this passage into French.

> Remember, these are quantities.

This morning I'm very organised. I am going to buy some bottles of mineral water, some cans of coke and lots of crisps. I'm organising a party this evening for my friend Anna. She is quite shy and really nervous but it is going to be fun.

> Note that the friend is called Anna.

> Remember that these are adjectives and may need to agree.

_____

_____

_____

_____

Adverbs   Forming adverbs

» *Foundation pp. 120–121*
» *Higher p. 129*

(G) An adverb is a word which describes a verb, telling you <u>how</u> something is done. It is important for you to be able to use adverbs, as they add precision and variety to what you write.

In English they often end in '–ly' (e.g. slow**ly**, noisi**ly**) and in French they often end in **–ment** (e.g. *heureusement*, *rapidement*), but there are plenty of exceptions.

Forming adverbs

To make an adverb, you often add **–ment** to the feminine form of an adjective:

masculine form of adjective	feminine form of adjective	adverb	English meaning
heureux	heureuse	heureusement	fortunately/happily
doux	douce	doucement	quietly/softly

However, some adjectives do not follow this pattern:

> *vrai* → *vraiment*   real/really
> *absolu* → *absolument*   absolute/absolutely

Some adverbs end in **emment**:

> *évident* → *évidemment*   obvious/obviously

Some adverbs end in **–amment**:

> *suffisant* (sufficient) → *suffisamment*   sufficiently
> *constant* (constant) → *constamment*   constantly

Some common adverbs are completely irregular:

> *bien* (well)   *Elle joue **bien**.*   She plays well.
> *mal* (badly)   *Il joue **mal**.*   He plays badly.
> *vite* (quickly)   *Elle parle **vite**.*   She speaks quickly.

Position

Adverbs can be placed in a number of places in a sentence. They often come just after the verb they describe, but you can put them elsewhere for emphasis, e.g. at the start of the sentence.

> *Je mange lentement.*   I eat slowly.   *Évidemment il est malade.*   Obviously he is ill.

1 **Form the adverbs from these adjectives.**

1 probable................

2 final................

3 seul................

4 général................

5 régulier................

6 naturel................

⭐ You will need to know the feminine form of the adjectives for these exercises.

2 **Replace the adjective with the correct form of the adverb.**

1 Je joue .... (*mauvais*).

2 Elle mange .... (*vite*).

3 Nous parlons .... (*doux*).

4 Vous marchez .... (*lent*).

5 Ils jouent .... (*bon*).

6 Tu pleures .... (*constant*).

3 **These adverbs have been formed incorrectly. Write the correct form of the adverb.**

1 Je joue ~~mauvaisement~~ .... au foot.

2 Elle joue ~~bonnement~~ .... du violon.

3 Il court ~~vitement~~ ....

4 C'est ~~vraiement~~ .... délicieux.

5 Nous parlons ~~douxment~~ ....

6 C'est ~~absoluement~~ .... super.

Studio GCSE French © Pearson Education Limited 2016

4 Choose the correct adjective or adverb to complete the sentences.

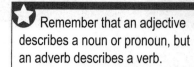

⭐ Remember that an adjective describes a noun or pronoun, but an adverb describes a verb.

1 Je joue *bon / bien* au foot.

2 Elle est très *heureuse / heureusement.*

3 Nous mangeons *lent / lentement.*

4 Il est *seul / seulement.*

5 Vous parlez *doux / doucement.*

6 Ils sont *timides / timidement.*

7 Elle finit *rapide / rapidement* ses devoirs.

8 Je suis *triste / tristement.*

5 Translate these sentences into English.

1 Je dors suffisamment en semaine.

2 Nous travaillons lentement en classe.

3 Je vais probablement faire de la natation.

4 On voyage vite en avion.

5 Elle joue mal du violon.

6 Il est vraiment grand.

7 Actuellement ma sœur évite le sucre.

Careful, this is a false friend!

6 Translate these sentences into French.

1 His mother only speaks Spanish.

Think about the word order here. Where will the adverb go?

2 He is really sad.

3 They are constantly late.

Ⓗ 7 Translate this passage into French.

Our cat disappears regularly but he normally comes home. I hear a noise in the garden, I open the door slowly and he comes in quickly. Fortunately he is happy and he is probably going to go out again.

Where will you put 'slowly'?

This could also be translated as 'happily'.

The adverb 'probably' will go between 'is going' and 'to go out' in French.

(G) You can make comparisons using **plus**, **moins** and **aussi...que** with adverbs in the same way you do with adjectives. This is useful if you want to compare two or more ways in which <u>things are done</u>.

To make a comparison with adverbs, just put *plus/moins/aussi* in front of the adverb and *que* after it.

*Tu parles **plus** lentement **que** lui.*	You speak **more** slowly **than** him.
*Vous mangez **moins** vite **que** moi.*	You eat **less** quickly **than** me.
*Elle joue **aussi** bien **que** ma sœur.*	She plays **as** well **as** my sister.

(H) There are plenty of exceptions to this rule, e.g. *bien* (well), *mal* (badly).

- The comparative form of *bien* (well) is *mieux* (better).
- The comparative form of *mal* (badly) is *pire* (worse).

*Elle joue **mieux que** mon ami.*   She plays **better than** my friend.

1 Match up the French and the English phrases.

1 Je mange plus lentement que toi.
2 Ils travaillent plus vite que moi.
3 Elle mange plus sainement que lui.
4 Il chante aussi bien que mon copain.
5 Nous parlons moins doucement que lui.
6 Tu joues du piano plus facilement que moi.

a They work more quickly than me.
b He sings as well as my friend.
c I eat more slowly than you.
d She eats more healthily than him.
e You play the piano more easily than me.
f We speak less softly than him.

2 Complete the sentences with the correct French word(s).

1 Elle chante _____ (*as well as*) moi.

2 Ils mangent_____ (*more healthily than*) mes amis.

3 Je mange _____ (*less slowly*) que toi.

4 Vous travaillez _____ (*harder*) que mon cousin.

(H) 5 Il joue _____ (*better*) que ma copine.

3 Write these sentences out in the correct order. Then translate them into English.

1 court moins que Elle vite vous _____

2 le train vite plus va que vélo Le _____

3 aussi chantes Tu que ta bien copine _____

(H) 4 mieux que dessine Je toi _____

(H) 5 joue piano Elle moi que mieux du _____

4 Translate these sentences into French.

1 She runs more quickly than me. _____

2 He sings louder than you. _____

> 'loud' is *fort* in French.

3 You speak French less fluently than me. _____

Studio GCSE French © Pearson Education Limited 2016

Adverbs Superlative adverbs

G You can use superlatives with adverbs to say something is done the quick<u>est</u>, <u>most</u> carefully, <u>best</u>, <u>least</u> elegantly, etc. For superlatives with adverbs you simply add *le plus* or *le moins,* followed by the adverb.

*Il a fini le travail **le plus** vite.*   He finished the work the **quickest**.
*Elle parle **le plus** lentement.*   She speaks the **slowest**.

H But remember that this rule doesn't apply to *mieux* or *pire*.

*Je joue **le mieux**.*   I play **the best**.

1 Complete the sentences with the correct superlative form.

Example: Le train va vite mais l'avion va le plus vite.

1 Je mange lentement mais ma copine mange ....

2 Vous mangez sainement mais mon père mange ....

3 Elles marchent vite mais je marche ....

4 Il fait rarement du judo mais elle fait du judo ....

5 Elle chante fort mais vous chantez ....

H 6 Tu joues bien au foot mais Ronaldo joue ....

2 Translate these sentences into English.

1 Mon père conduit le plus vite. ....

2 Mon petit frère lit le plus lentement. ....

3 Un vélo roule le plus vite. ....

4 Elle mange le moins poliment. ....

> Can you guess what this means?

H 3 Translate these sentences into French.

1 Paul writes the best. ....

2 He runs the quickest. ....

3 I speak the slowest. ....

> ⭐ Remember that the superlative form is *le plus* or *le moins* plus the correct adverb.

H 4 Translate this passage into French.

> ⭐ You will need to use the comparative and superlative forms in this translation.

> Think carefully about the word for 'me' here.

My friend Céline plays the piano better than me, but my friend Alice plays the best. I would like to play better than her but I also want to play the quickest. However, I eat more healthily and I do sport more regularly than my friends.

....

....

....

Adverbs   Interrogative adverbs

» Foundation p. 15
» Higher p. 57

G Interrogative adverbs are question words such as 'How?', 'When?', 'Why?', which are used to ask for new information or facts. The most common French interrogative adverbs are:

combien (de)	**how many/much**	
Combien de livres veux-tu?	How many books do you want?	
comment	**how, what**	
C'était comment?	What was it like? / How was it?	
où	**where**	
Où habites-tu?	Where do you live?	
pourquoi	**why**	
Pourquoi aimes-tu le foot?	Why do you like football?	
quand	**when**	
Quand est-ce que tu pars?	When are you leaving?	

There are three ways to ask a question in French.

1. Put the question word at the end and raise the tone of your voice (or add a question mark):
   Tu habites où?

2. Put the question word at the start and add **est-ce que**:
   Où est-ce que tu habites?

3. Invert the subject and verb after the question word:
   Où habites-tu?

1 Complete the sentences with an appropriate interrogative adverb.

1 Tu as _____ frères et sœurs?

2 _____ as-tu voyagé?

3 _____ habites-tu?

4 Tu t'appelles _____ ?

5 _____ est-ce que tu aimes nager?

⭐ There could be more than one possible question for each answer.

2 Write a question to go with each answer.

Example: J'aime le dessin car c'est créatif. *Pourquoi est-ce que tu aimes le dessin?*

1 J'arrive au collège à huit heures. _____

2 Je m'appelle Lucas. _____

3 J'ai deux frères et une sœur. _____

4 J'habite en Suisse. _____

5 Le voyage était intéressant. _____

3 Translate these sentences into French.

1 How many friends have you got?

You will have to use a part of *avoir*.

_____

2 Where does your aunt live?

_____

3 Why does he like reading on the Kindle?

_____

Studio GCSE French © Pearson Education Limited 2016

Adverbs   Adverbs of time, frequency and place

(G) There are also many other very useful adverbs which describe <u>how often</u>, <u>when</u> and <u>where</u> an action is done, which you could use to enhance your written and spoken French. Here are some examples:

adverbs of frequency (how often)		adverbs of time (when)		adverbs of place (where)	
toujours	always	*aujourd'hui*	today	*ici*	here
souvent	often	*hier*	yesterday	*là-bas*	over there
d'habitude	usually	*demain*	tomorrow	*loin*	far
normalement	normally	*enfin, finalement*	at last, finally	*partout*	everywhere
quelquefois	sometimes	*d'abord*	at first, firstly		
de temps	from time to	*dans le futur*	in the future		
en temps	time	*déjà*	already		
rarement	rarely	*tout de suite*	immediately		
		maintenant	now		
		plus tard	later		

> ⭐ • Adverbs of frequency are usually placed after the verb.
> • Adverbs of time can often go at the beginning or end of the sentence in French.

1 **Underline the adverb in these sentences.**

1 J'ai déjà fait cela.

2 Je vais partir demain.

3 Ils habitent ici depuis deux ans.

4 Plus tard, on va au ciné.

5 Normalement je vais au collège à pied.

6 Nous jouons au foot de temps en temps.

2 **Match up the French and the English phrases.**

1 J'ai joué au foot hier.

2 Je vais rarement au musée.

3 D'abord c'était difficile.

4 Nous sommes partis tout de suite.

5 Je joue souvent au volley.

a I often play volleyball.

b I played football yesterday.

c We left immediately.

d I rarely go to the museum.

e At first it was difficult.

3 **Translate these sentences into English.**

1 D'habitude je vais en vacances en Suisse.

2 Je vais quelquefois au cinéma.

3 Nous sommes enfin arrivés en France.

4 Maintenant je ne joue plus au badminton.

> ⭐ Make sure you put the adverb in the correct place in English so that the sentences make sense.

> Remember that *ne… plus* means 'no longer' or 'anymore'.

4 **Translate these sentences into French. Each contains at least one adverb.**

1 Today I'm going to play on my computer.

2 We are going swimming later.

3 He often listens to music.

> Remember, 'I'm going' is the same as 'I go' in French.

> Think about the word order in French.

Pronouns   Subject pronouns

(G) Subject pronouns are at the heart of every verb you use in French, so it is really important to be familiar with them.

The <u>subject</u> is the person or thing which does the action of the verb. The subject can be a <u>noun</u> (e.g. 'the girls') or a <u>pronoun</u> (e.g. 'they'). In the sentence, '**I** download music', the pronoun '**I**' is the subject.

Every verb can have a pronoun as its subject:

je	I	shortens to *j'* before a vowel or h
tu	you	for a child, young person, friend or animal!
il	he/it	means *it* when replacing a masculine noun
elle	she/it	means *it* when replacing a feminine noun
on	one/we/you	often used in French instead of *nous*
nous	we	
vous	you	used for more than one person, or someone you don't know very well
ils	they	used for masculine nouns or a mixed group
elles	they	used for feminine nouns

⭐ Note that *je* changes to *j'* before a vowel or silent *h*: *j'aime* (I like).

Tu and *vous*

You will see that there are two words for 'you'. You use **tu** when you are being friendly or informal, addressing members of your family or people of roughly your age or younger. You use **vous** when you are being polite or formal, with people you don't know or who are much older than you and when there is more than one person.

> *Bonjour, je peux **vous** aider?* — Hello, can I help **you**?
> *Je vais faire du roller, veux-**tu** venir?* — I am going roller skating, do **you** want to come?

In French, the subject pronoun **on** is also frequently used. It literally translates as 'one', but this seems very posh in English, so you might translate *on* as 'you' or 'we', depending on the context:

> ***On** va en ville le samedi.* — **We** go into town on Saturdays.
> ***On** peut faire les magasins.* — **You** can go shopping.

On uses the same part of the verb as *il* and *elle*: the third person singular.

Here is the verb *aller* in the present tense with the nine different subject pronouns used:

je vais	I go / am going	*nous allons*	we go / are going
tu vas	you go / are going	*vous allez*	you go / are going
il va	he goes / is going	*ils vont*	they go / are going
elle va	she goes / is going	*elles vont*	they go / are going
on va	one goes / is going		

1 **Choose the correct subject pronoun to go with each verb.**

1 *je / nous* aimons le foot
2 *elle / elles* aiment lire
3 *vous / ils* aimez les chats
4 *je / tu* détestes faire tes devoirs
5 *on / elles* déteste faire du camping
6 *je / vous* déteste faire de la danse

2 **Match up the French and the English.**

1 je mange   a we go
2 nous allons   b you like
3 vous détestez   c they go
4 tu aimes   d you hate
5 ils vont   e I eat

Studio GCSE French © Pearson Education Limited 2016

3 **Replace the nouns with the correct French subject pronoun. Then translate the sentences into English.**

1 ~~Marc~~ .... va au collège à pied.

....

2 ~~Ma mère~~ .... est très intelligente.

....

3 ~~Les garçons~~ .... sont toujours méchants et quelquefois égoïstes.

....

4 ~~Sylvie et Sophie~~ .... vont en ville ensemble.

....

5 ~~Mes copains et moi~~ .... allons souvent au cinéma voir des films comiques.

....

> Remember that it's 'My friends and I'.

4 **Translate these sentences into French.**

1 She hates swimming and horse riding.

> Translate 'swimming' and 'horse riding' as nouns here.

....

2 We are sending an email.

....

3 Do you like flowers?

> Use the normal word order and just add a question mark.

....

Ⓗ 5 **Translate this passage into French.**

> In French we say 'a concert of music rock'.

Yesterday I went to a rock music concert with my friends. Adrienne and Gabrielle prefer classical music but the concert was great. I often go to the cinema with my sister. We usually go at the weekend. She likes horror movies but I love action films because they are exciting. What do you like to do?

> This usually comes after the verb in French.

....

....

....

....

....

....

(G) These pronouns have specific uses in French, so it is important for you to be able to use them and recognise them too.

moi	me	*nous*	us
toi	you	*vous*	you
lui	him, it	*eux*	them (m)
elle	her, it	*elles*	them (f)

They can be used:

- for emphasis of the subject of a verb:

  Moi, je n'aime pas les films. I don't like films. / As for **me**, I don't like films.

- for compound (more than one) subjects:

  Toi et moi allons en ville demain. **You** and **I** are going into town tomorrow.

- to stand alone:

  Qui a parlé? Moi. Who spoke? **Me**.

- after a preposition or after *ne … que* (only):

  avec moi with **me**   *après toi* after **you**

  Je n'ai vu qu'elle. I only saw **her**.   *sans elle* without **her**

- after the expressions *être à*, *faire attention à* or *penser à*:

  C'est à moi. It's **mine**.   *Je pense à eux.* I'm thinking of **them**.

- after **chez** (at the house of):

  Je mange chez elle. I'm eating **at** her house.

- after *que* in comparisons:

  Je suis plus grand que toi. I'm taller **than** you.

1 Choose the correct emphatic pronoun to translate the English.

1 except me – sauf *moi / elle*

2 for you – pour *eux / toi*

3 in spite of him – malgré *lui / elle*

4 with them – avec *elle / elles*

5 after us – après *nous / vous*

6 before her – avant *lui / elle*

2 Replace the nouns with the correct emphatic pronoun.

1 Je m'entends bien avec ~~mon frère~~ ....

2 Elle pense à ~~sa mère~~ ....

3 Il était là avant ~~ses copains~~ ....

4 Vous allez au café avec ~~Amélie et Louise~~ ....

5 Tu es derrière ~~ton copain~~ ....

6 Je suis chez ~~ma copine~~ ....

7 Elle est plus grande que ~~son frère~~ ....

8 Je suis moins intelligent que ~~mes sœurs~~ ....

que will change to *qu'* before a vowel.

3 Complete the sentences with the correct French emphatic pronoun.

1 Je vais arriver à la gare routière après _____ . (*you, plural*)

2 Elle est triste sans _____ . (*him*)

3 Il y a un paquet pour _____ à la poste. (*her*)

4 Vous pensez souvent à _____ . (*them, feminine*)

5 Ils se sont cachés derrière _____ . (*them, masculine*)

6 Tu as quitté le collège avant _____ . (*me*)

4 Translate the following sentences into English.

1 Il va rester chez nous. _____

2 Je vais en vacances sans toi. _____

3 Toi et moi allons jouer au badminton. _____

4 Ce livre est à moi. _____

5 Lui, il aime le foot. _____

5 Translate these sentences into French.

1 There is an email for you.

_____

> There could be two options for 'you' here.

2 I would like to go to France with her.

_____

> 'Always' comes after 'arrive' in French.

3 We always arrive after them.

_____

H 6 Translate this passage into French.

> Remember that this is *là* in French.

> This will be an infinitive in French.

My best friend is called Mark. I get on well with him because he is always there for me. He and I do everything together. On Sundays we meet our friends in town and play rugby with them. Mark likes playing golf but I prefer playing the guitar. What about you? Do you play a musical instrument?

> Don't forget there is a preposition that follows 'to play' when talking about a musical instrument.

_____

_____

_____

_____

_____

_____

_____

G Relative pronouns are words like 'who', 'which' and 'whose'. They relate back to someone or something that has just been mentioned.

The two most common ones are *qui* and *que*. They help create longer, more complex sentences in French.

- **qui** means 'who' or 'which' and is the <u>subject</u> of the clause.

*J'ai une sœur **qui** s'appelle Éloise.*	I have a sister **who** is called Éloise.
*Ma sœur, **qui** a dix ans, est très mignonne.*	My sister, **who** is 10, is very cute.

- **Que** means 'whom' or 'which' and is the <u>object</u> of the clause. It changes to *qu'* before a vowel or silent 'h'.

*Le chien **que** j'ai vu était gris.*	The dog **which** I saw was grey. ('I' is the subject of the verb, so the dog is the object.)
*L'homme **que** j'ai remarqué dans la rue portait une écharpe noire.*	The man, **whom** I noticed in the street, was wearing a black scarf.

H dont

Dont means 'whose/of whom/about whom' and is used in a similar way.

*La fille **dont** j'ai parlé.*	The girl **of whom** I have spoken.
*Le film **dont** j'ai aimé la bande sonore.*	The film **whose** soundtrack I liked.

However, you do not need to be able to use it yourself; you just need to recognise it.

1 **Link the sentences together using *qui*.**

Example: Ma copine s'appelle Noémie. Elle est très intelligente.

<u>Ma copine, qui s'appelle Noémie, est très intelligente.</u>

1 Mon frère s'appelle Luc. Il est assez sportif.

_____

2 Mon ami est actif. Il joue souvent au foot.

_____

3 Ma mère aime faire du vélo. Elle est en bonne forme.

_____

4 Son père va souvent à la pêche. Il aime être tranquille.

_____

5 Sa copine ne mange jamais de chocolat. Elle est très mince.

_____

H 2 **Choose the correct word. *Qui* or *que*?**

1 L'homme *qui* / *que* je connais est très sympa.

2 C'est Karine *qui* / *que* est la plus intelligente.

3 Mon copain, *qui* / *que* s'appelle Alain, est bavard.

4 Le musée *qui* / *que* j'ai visité était intéressant.

5 Mes parents, *qui* / *que* j'adore, sont vraiment gentils.

6 Où est le livre *qui* / *que* j'ai acheté hier?

H 3 **Fill in the gaps with *qui*, *que* or *qu'*.**

1 L'homme _____ est allé en ville porte une veste bleue.

2 Le chien _____ j'ai vu était énorme.

3 Quel est le film _____ il voudrait voir?

4 Ma copine, _____ s'appelle Lucie, a seize ans.

5 Voilà le chapeau _____ elle a perdu.

6 Le roman _____ j'ai acheté était barbant.

Studio GCSE French © Pearson Education Limited 2016

Pronouns   Interrogative pronouns

G *Qui* can also be an interrogative pronoun (question word) meaning 'who' or 'whom'. It is used when asking about people. When 'whom' is the object of the question, *qui* can be followed by *est-ce que*, or you can change the order of the verb and subject.

Qui parle?	**Who** is speaking?
Qui vois-tu? or *Qui est-ce que tu vois?*	**Who(m)** do you see?

Qui can also be used after a preposition:

Tu parles à qui?	To **whom** are you speaking?

Que means 'what' and is used to refer to ideas or things. When it is used as the object of the question, it can be followed by *est-ce que* or you can invert the verb.

Que penses-tu du film? or *Qu'est-ce que tu penses du film?*   **What** do you think of the film?

1 Match up the English and French questions.

1	Qui est là?		a	What is it?
2	Que fais-tu le soir?		b	Who is there?
3	Qu'est-ce que tu aimes faire?		c	Who does the cooking in your house?
4	Qui fait la cuisine chez toi?		d	What do you like doing?
5	Qu'est-ce que c'est?		e	What do you do in the evenings?

> ⭐ Even though we sometimes leave out the relative pronoun in English, it must always be there in French:
> *l'homme **que** je connais*
> the man I know / the man <u>whom</u> I know

2 Translate these sentences into English.

1 Le repas que nous avons pris au restaurant était délicieux.

2 Le parapluie qu'elle a perdu était rouge.

3 L'homme qui habite près de chez moi est très sportif.

3 Translate these sentences into French.

> No word for 'is' here.

1 The man who is arriving is my uncle.

2 I have a brother who is called Luc.

3 My friend, who likes swimming, is going to the seaside.

> 'Swimming' will be an infinitive here.

H 4 Now translate this passage into French.

My friend, who is called Justine, likes chatting on the internet. Her father, whom I know, is very famous. He gets on well with the woman who was singing on TV last night. She sang the song which you like.

> This is the imperfect tense: no word for 'was' here.

> Past tense here: perfect or imperfect?

(G) Pronouns are used to replace nouns. The object is the person or thing which receives the action of the verb.

Direct object pronouns are used when the noun is not the subject of the sentence: 'she loves **him**'; 'I watched **them**'.

me	me	*nous*	us
te	you	*vous*	you
le	him/it	*les*	them
la	her/it		

Note: *le* and *la* change to *l'* before a vowel or silent 'h'.

In French, the object pronoun comes in front of the verb.

*Nous **les** voyons.*	We see **them**.
*Il **l'**envoie.*	He sends **it**.
*Ils **nous** invitent.*	They invite **us**.

In a negative sentence, the pronoun remains immediately in front of the verb.

*Je ne **l'**aime pas.*	I don't like **it**.

In the perfect tense, the pronoun comes in front of the auxiliary verb (normally a part of *avoir*).

*Je **l'**ai regardé.*	I watched **it**.

In the near future tense, the pronoun comes after the auxiliary verb.

(H) However, in the perfect and pluperfect tenses the past participle must agree with the object pronoun, adding an 'e' for the feminine, 's' for masculine plural and 'es' for feminine plural. This is known as a preceding direct object or PDO.

*Je **l'**ai vue.*	I saw **her**.
*Je **les** ai vus.*	I saw **them**.

Using pronouns is essential, as it prevents the need to repeat nouns or names and will make your language sound more natural. Object pronouns are useful as they involve a different word order in French, so it is a sign of your awareness of structure if you can use them correctly.

1 Circle the direct object pronoun and then translate the following sentences into English.

1 Je la regarde. ....

2 Nous te voyons. ....

3 Je vais les voir. ....

> Note that the pronoun comes between *vais* and *voir*.

4 Elle l'achète. ....

5 Nous allons vous chercher. ....

(H) 2 Replace the underlined noun with a pronoun and put it in the correct position in the sentence.

Example: Elle lit <u>le journal</u>.   Elle le lit.

1 Vous cherchez <u>le portable</u>. ....

2 Tu regardes <u>la télé</u>? ....

3 Nous envoyons <u>les e-mails</u>. ....

4 Je vais trouver <u>mon copain</u>. ....

5 Elle attend <u>son amie</u>. ....

6 Elles ont vu <u>les émissions</u>. ....

> ⭐ Remember that object pronouns go in front of the verb. In sentence 6 there is a preceding direct object in the perfect tense so take care!

(G) Indirect object pronouns are used to say 'to me', '<u>to</u> him', and so on.

me	to/for me	*nous*	to/for us
te	to/for you	*vous*	to/for you
lui	to/for him/her	*leur*	to/for them

They are used with verbs like **donner**, **dire**, **parler**, **demander** and **téléphoner**, which are followed by *à* + a noun.

*Je **lui** envoie un texto.*   I'm sending a text **to him**.   *Je **leur** ai donné une lettre.*   I gave a letter **to them**.

Indirect object pronouns follow the same rules regarding their position in the sentence as direct object pronouns, but there is no agreement of the past participle in the perfect and pluperfect tenses.

In English we sometimes miss out the word 'to' (I gave him it). This cannot happen in French as *lui* would be needed here, so you need to remember to use an indirect object pronoun when you actually mean '<u>to</u> him'.

Order of direct and indirect object pronouns

When you have *le/la/les* (direct object pronouns) and *lui/leur* (indirect object pronouns) in the same sentence, *le/la/les* comes first.

*Je **le lui** ai donné.*   I gave **it to him**.

(H) 1 **Rewrite the sentences, replacing the underlined word with the correct pronoun.**

1   Je parle <u>à mon ami</u>. _____

2   Elle téléphone <u>à la police</u>. _____

3   Nous donnons de l'argent <u>aux enfants</u>. _____

4   Il a parlé <u>à des amis</u>. _____

> Remember that *aux* tells you that the following word is plural.

> Remember that the pronoun comes in front of the part of *avoir*.

(H) 2 **Complete these sentences.**

1   I'm sending it (m) to them. → Je _____ envoie.

2   He gave them to her. → Il _____ a donnés.

3   We are going to send it (f) to him. → Nous allons _____ envoyer.

4   I'm going to give them to him. → Je vais _____ donner.

5   They telephone them every day. → Ils _____ téléphonent tous les jours.

> ⭐ Remember that the direct object comes before the indirect object.

3 **Translate these sentences into English.**

1   Il nous a envoyé un message. _____

2   Je ne l'ai pas regardé. _____

3   Paul leur a parlé hier. _____

4   Mes parents m'ont acheté une voiture. _____

5   Je t'ai vu en ville. _____

(H) 4 **Translate the following sentences into French.**

1   He sees us every morning. _____

2   I don't understand it. _____

3   They speak to her online. _____

4   I phoned her yesterday. _____

> ⭐ You need to decide whether to use a direct or indirect object pronoun. Does the noun it is replacing have *à* in front of it?

> Remember that the pronoun still comes immediately before the verb, even when there is a negative.

Pronouns Indefinite, demonstrative and possessive pronouns

>> Higher p. 108

G Indefinite pronouns

Indefinite pronouns don't refer to a specific noun, so they do not change. The only one you need to know and use is **quelqu'un** (someone). It works in a similar way to 'someone' in English. It can replace the subject or object in a sentence or can be used after a preposition. It is used with the third person singular form of the verb.

Quelqu'un a téléphoné.   **Someone** rang.
J'ai un cadeau pour quelqu'un.   I have a present for **someone**.

Demonstrative pronouns

The demonstrative pronouns you need to learn and use are words that can be used to mean 'that'. The quick and easy way to say 'that' is to use **cela** or **ça**, which can both mean 'that' as the subject or object of a sentence. They are both used with the third person singular (*il/elle/on*) form of the verb. Using them will help you sound more natural and fluent in French.

Cela me fait plaisir.   **That** makes me happy.   *Qui a fait ça?*   Who did **that**?

H You also need to recognise the demonstrative pronouns that mean 'this one/that one/these ones/those ones'. They must agree with the gender and number of the noun they replace. They are used when you want to make it clear which noun you are talking about, for example, when you are choosing something: 'I like this one; do you prefer that one?'

masculine singular	feminine singular	masculine plural	feminine plural
celui	celle	ceux	celles

You can add *–ci* or *–là* to the end of the noun to distinguish between '<u>this</u> one' and '<u>that</u> one'.

celui-ci   **this** one (m)   *celle-là*   **that** one (f)

Demonstrative pronouns can also mean 'the one(s)' or 'those' and are often followed by *qui* or *que*.

Pour ceux qui aiment le sport, …   For **those** who like sport, …

H Possessive pronouns

Possessive pronouns translate the English 'mine', 'yours', etc. and the form used agrees with the noun it refers to. You won't have to use them yourself but you will need to be able to recognise them.

masculine singular	feminine singular	masculine plural	feminine plural	English meaning
le mien	la mienne	les miens	les miennes	mine
le tien	la tienne	les tiens	les tiennes	yours
le sien	la sienne	les siens	les siennes	his/hers/its
le nôtre	la nôtre	les nôtres		ours
le vôtre	la vôtre	les vôtres		yours
le leur	la leur	les leurs		theirs

C'est le mien.   It's **mine**.
Voilà ma maison. Où est la tienne?   There's my house. Where's **yours**?

1 Match up the French and English sentences.

1 Il y a quelqu'un à la porte.   **a** That makes me laugh.

2 Cela me fait rire.   **b** Who said that?

3 Qui a dit ça?   **c** I don't like that.

4 Je n'aime pas ça.   **d** Someone has arrived.

5 Quelqu'un est arrivé.   **e** There's someone at the door.

2 Complete the sentences with the correct word in French.

1 _____ (*That*) est important.

2 Tu aimes beaucoup _____ (*that*).

3 Nous avons vu _____ (*someone*) devant l'église.

4 Elle déteste _____ (*that*) car c'est barbant.

5 _____ (*Someone*) nous a vus dans le parc.

Studio GCSE French © Pearson Education Limited 2016

H 3 Complete the sentences with the the correct word in French.

1 _____ (*Someone*) est arrivé en retard.

2 Nous avons deux vélos. _____ (*This one*) est rouge.

3 J'ai acheté deux billets de ciné. _____ (*That one*) était plus cher.

4 J'ai vu trois ordinateurs dans le magasin. Je préfère _____ (*those*) qui sont plus petits.

5 J'ai deux nouvelles chemises. Je préfère _____ (*the one*) de gauche.

H 4 Choose the correct answer to complete each sentence.

1 Il y a deux romans. Celui-ci est *le mien / la mienne.*

2 Je vois deux voitures devant la maison. Celle-là est *le sien / la sienne.*

3 Il y a des chaussures dans le salon. Celles-ci sont *les tiens / les tiennes.*

4 J'ai remarqué des gants dans la salle à manger. Lesquels sont *les siens / les siennes?*

5 Tu vois les deux chiens? Celui-là est *le leur / la leur.*

6 Voilà deux portables. Celui-ci est *le nôtre / la nôtre.*

5 Translate these sentences into English.

1 Je trouve ça très intéressant. _____

2 Il y a quelqu'un dans la maison. _____

H 3 J'aime celui-ci mieux que celui-là. _____

H 4 Je préfère celle que j'ai vue hier. _____

H 5 Ce portable est le tien. _____

6 Translate these sentences into French.

1 I don't want that. _____

2 There is someone in the street. _____

3 What does that mean? _____

> Remember that the negative goes around the verb.

> 'Mean' is translated by two verbs in French; the second one is in the infinitive.

H 7 Translate this passage into English.

> This is in the imperfect tense but how will you translate it?

Ce matin il y avait quelqu'un dans notre jardin. Ma mère a trouvé ça inquiétant. Plus tard j'ai vu deux hommes. Celui de gauche portait de belles fleurs. C'étaient celles de notre jardin. J'ai crié, « Ces fleurs sont les nôtres ».

> Don't translate *les*.

> This is also an imperfect tense. Will you translate it differently here?

_____

_____

_____

_____

» *Foundation p. 97, p. 100*
» *Higher p. 58, pp. 78–79*

G *y* and *en* are common words that are used to replace nouns that have already been mentioned.

y

y usually means 'there' or 'to there'. You use *y* to refer to a place which has already been mentioned, e.g. *à la maison* or *en ville*, and it comes before the verb. It is not always needed in English, but you must include it in French.

Tu vas à la gare? Oui, j'y vais.	Are you going **to the station**? Yes, I'm going **there**.
J'aime aller à Londres. Moi aussi, j'aime y aller.	I like going **to London**. Me too, I like going **there**.

y often replaces *à* + **a noun** or **place name** and is used with verbs which are followed by *à*.

Tu joues au golf? Oui, j'y joue.	Do you play golf? Yes, I play (**it**).

en

This little word can have a number of meanings, including 'some', 'any', 'of it' and 'of them', so it is a good one to know! You use it to replace *du*, *de la*, *de l'* or *des* and a noun which has already been mentioned.

Tu veux du thé? Oui, j'en veux bien.	Do you want some tea? Yes, I'd like **some**.

It is also used with expressions of quantity, such as beaucoup, often to mean 'of it' or 'of them' when we would not include such a word in English.

Tu as combien de frères? J'en ai deux.	How many **brothers** do you have? I have two (**of them**).
Tu manges du poisson? Oui, j'en mange beaucoup.	Do you eat **fish**? Yes, I eat a lot (**of it**).

It's not just after quantities that you might use *en* in French when it wouldn't be needed in English. It is also used to replace *de* + **a word**, sometimes after a verb which requires *de*.

Tu joue du piano? Oui, j'en joue.	Do you play the piano? Yes, I play (it).

Like other object pronouns, *y* and *en* come <u>before</u> the verb in the present tense. In the perfect tense, they come before the part of *avoir* or *être*.

Les États-Unis? *J'y suis allée l'année dernière.*	**America?** I went **there** last year.
On a mangé du gâteau. J'en ai gardé une tranche pour toi.	We ate **some** cake. I kept a slice **of it** for you.

1 Translate the questions and answers into English.

1. Des fraises? J'en ai mangé beaucoup.

2. Le cinéma Odéon? J'y suis allé voir un film anglais.

3. Le cyclisme? Il en fait de temps en temps.

4. La guitare? Elle en joue des fois.

2 Underline the noun to which *en* or *y* refers.

Example: Tu as de l'<u>argent</u>? Non, je n'en ai pas.

1. Avez-vous des sœurs? Non, je n'en ai pas.
2. Tu as des bonbons? Oui, j'en ai beaucoup.
3. Tu manges du poisson? Non, je n'en mange pas.
4. Vous voulez des sandwichs? Oui, j'en veux bien.
5. Tu bois du coca? Non, je n'en bois pas.
6. Vous allez en France? Oui, j'y vais.

H 3 **Rewrite the sentences, replacing the underlined words with y.**

1 Je vais <u>en ville</u>.

2 Tu vas <u>au cinéma</u>.

3 Il est allé <u>à la piscine</u>.

4 Nous sommes allés <u>à New York</u>.

5 Ils vont <u>à la patinoire</u>.

> ⭐ Remember that y and en come in a different place in the sentence in French.

H 4 **Rewrite the sentences, replacing the underlined words with en.**

1 Tu voudrais <u>du café</u>?

2 Je mange <u>de la viande</u>.

3 J'ai acheté <u>des pommes</u>.

4 Vous avez <u>des bonbons</u>?

5 <u>Que</u> penses-tu <u>de</u> la question?

> Que becomes qu' before a vowel.

> It is penser de … here.

H 5 **Rewrite the sentences, replacing the underlined words with y or en.**

1 Je joue souvent <u>du violon</u>.

2 Je joue souvent <u>au rugby</u>.

3 On va <u>en France</u>.

4 Je voudrais <u>du sucre</u>.

5 Nous avons beaucoup <u>de choses</u>.

> ⭐ Remember that y comes before the part of être in the perfect tense.

H 6 **Translate these sentences into French.**

1 I have already been there.

2 Swimming? I do it every day.

3 Football? I play it regularly.

H 7 **Translate this passage into French.**

> 'Often' comes after 'go' in French.

> It is jouer du piano.

There is a theatre in town and I often go there with my friends. We went there last Saturday. A good friend goes there on Sundays to play the piano in a concert. He has been playing it for a year. I like going to the sports centre to play tennis. I played it yesterday.

> It is jouer au tennis.

> Think carefully about the tense here: how will you translate 'for a year'?

Verbs   The present tense: regular verbs

(G) The present tense is the most commonly used tense, so crack it and it's a great start!

There are three types of regular verbs (*–er*, *–ir* and *–re* verbs), but the most common are *–er* verbs.

To form the present tense of these regular verbs, cross off *–er*, *–ir* or *–re* and add the following endings:

	–er verbs	–ir verbs	–re verbs
je	–e	–is	–s
tu	–es	–is	–s
il/elle/on	–e	–it	–
nous	–ons	–issons	–ons
vous	–ez	–issez	–ez
ils/elles	–ent	–issent	–ent

In English we use the continuous present 'I am playing' as well as 'I play', but in French the present tense covers both of these meanings.

jouer	to play
je jou**e**	I play/am playing
tu jou**es**	you play/are playing
il/elle/on jou**e**	he/she/one plays/ is playing
nous jou**ons**	we play/are playing
vous jou**ez**	you play/are playing
ils/elles jou**ent**	they play/are playing

finir	to finish
je fin**is**	I finish/am finishing
tu fin**is**	you finish/are finishing
il/elle/on fin**it**	he/she/one finishes/ is finishing
nous fin**issons**	we finish/are finishing
vous fin**issez**	you finish/are finishing
ils/elles fin**issent**	they finish/are finishing

vendre	to sell
je vend**s**	I sell/am selling
tu vend**s**	you sell/are selling
il/elle/on vend	he/she/one sells/ is selling
nous vend**ons**	we sell/are selling
vous vend**ez**	you sell/are selling
ils vend**ent**	they sell/are selling

Some *–er* verbs have spelling changes:

- Verbs ending in *–ger* (e.g. *manger, nager*) add *–e* in the *nous* form to soften the g sound: *nous mangeons*.
- Verbs ending in *–ler* and *–ter* (e.g. *appeler, jeter*) double the *l* or the *t* in the *je, tu, il/elle/on* and *ils/elles* forms: *j'appelle, elle jette*.
- Verbs ending in *–yer* (e.g. *envoyer, payer*) change the *y* to *i* in the *je, tu, il/elle/on* and *ils/elles* forms: *tu envoies, ils paient*.
- Some verbs change *e* or *é* to *è* (e.g. *acheter – j'achète, préférer – je préfère*). This change only happens in the *je, tu, il/elle/on* and *ils/elles* forms.

1 Choose the correct form of the verb to complete each sentence.

1 Elle *joue / jouent* au foot.
2 Nous *finissez / finissons* à 15 heures.
3 Ils *achetent / achètent* du poisson.
4 Je *jette / jettes* le ballon.
5 Il *habites / habite* en France.
6 Vous *vend / vendez* des portables.

2 Put the verb in brackets into the correct form.

1 elles (*bavarder*) _____

2 nous (*manger*) _____

3 vous (*choisir*) _____

4 on (*répondre*) _____

5 tu (*envoyer*) _____

6 je (*porter*) _____

Studio GCSE French © Pearson Education Limited 2016

3 How would you say the following in French?

1 you (sg) live ....

2 we find ....

3 she plays ....

4 I sell ....

5 you (pl) finish ....

6 they (m) wait ....

4 Fill in the correct part of the verb and translate the sentences into English.

1 Ils .... (habiter) en Espagne.

....

2 Anna .... (préférer) le dessin à l'école.

....

3 Je .... (rougir) car je suis timide.

....

4 Les filles .... (attendre) leurs amis devant le cinéma.

....

5 Tu .... (aimer) le français?

....

6 Vous .... (nettoyer) la maison.

....

> ⭐ You use the *il/elle* form (he/she) when it is someone's name. When it is a plural noun (e.g. *les filles*), you use the *ils/elles* (they) form.

5 Translate these sentences into French.

1 My friend is choosing a present.

....

2 They tidy the bedrooms.

....

3 I am selling my bike.

....

> ⭐ There is no word for 'is' or 'are' in sentences like 'he is waiting' or 'they are talking' when you translate them into French. You just need the correct part of the present tense.

H 6 Now translate this passage into French.

What preposition do you need to use here?

We live in a village in the mountains. It snows a lot here. I play hockey and I swim at the sports centre. My friend finishes school at 3 p.m. and we eat in a restaurant near the station. In the evening, my family watches TV. Do you like TV?

Make sure you have the correct *nous* ending.

Remember that 'near' is *près de*.

....

....

....

....

....

Ⓖ Irregular verbs follow no fixed pattern so you need to learn them separately. They are really important as they are very common. The four most common irregular present tense verbs are:

avoir (to have)	*être* (to be)	*aller* (to go)	*faire* (to do / make)
j'ai	je suis	je vais	je fais
tu as	tu es	tu vas	tu fais
il/elle/on a	il/elle/on est	il/elle/on va	il/elle/on fait
nous avons	nous sommes	nous allons	nous faisons
vous avez	vous êtes	vous allez	vous faites
ils/elles ont	ils/elles sont	ils/elles vont	ils/elles font

- *Avoir* is used in many phrases such as:

J'*ai* mal à la tête.	I **have** a headache.

  but also in cases where we would use a different verb in English:

J'*ai* tort.	I **am** wrong.
J'*ai* seize ans.	I **am** 16.

- *Être* is also used frequently in phrases:

Je **suis** anglais.	I'**m** English.
C'**est** super.	It **is** great.

- *Aller* is useful to express the idea of going:

Je **vais** en ville.	I **go** into town.
Mon frère **va** au cinéma.	My brother **goes** to the cinema.

- *Faire* is used in many expressions, including the weather:

Il **fait** chaud.	It **is** hot.

  and for talking about activities and sports:

Elle **fait** de la natation.	She **goes** swimming.
Nous **faisons** du VTT.	We **go** mountain biking.

Other common irregular verbs in the present tense are shown below.

prendre (to take)	*dire* (to say / tell)	*voir* (to see)	*rire* (to laugh)	*mettre* (to put)	*sortir* (to go out)
je prends	je dis	je vois	je ris	je mets	je sors
tu prends	tu dis	tu vois	tu ris	tu mets	tu sors
il/elle/on prend	il/elle/on dit	il/elle/on voit	il/elle/on rit	il/elle/on met	il/elle/on sort
nous prenons	nous disons	nous voyons	nous rions	nous mettons	nous sortons
vous prenez	vous dites	vous voyez	vous riez	vous mettez	vous sortez
ils/elles prennent	ils/elles disent	ils/elles voient	ils/elles rient	ils/elles mettent	ils/elles sortent

1 **Choose the correct part of the verb.**

1 Elle *fait / va* en ville le week-end.

2 Tu *as / es* des frères?

3 Elles *vont / font* du vélo.

4 Je *suis / J'ai* anglais.

5 Vous *prenons / prenez* un repas au café.

6 Nous *rions / rient* beaucoup.

2 **Write the correct part of the verb in brackets.**

1 nous (*sortir*) ....

2 vous (*avoir*) ....

3 il (*être*) ....

4 je (*faire*) ....

5 ils (*mettre*) ....

6 on (*prendre*) ....

7 tu (*dire*) ....

8 elle (*voir*) ....

9 les garçons (*rire*) ....

10 elles (*aller*) ....

Studio GCSE French © Pearson Education Limited 2016

3 Put the verb in brackets into the present tense and then translate the sentence into English.

1 Vous _____ (*aller*) à la pêche.

_____

2 Marie et Nicole _____ (*faire*) du ski.

_____

3 Nous _____ (*prendre*) un repas au restaurant.

_____

4 Ils _____ (*sortir*) à neuf heures.

_____

5 Tu _____ (*rire*) beaucoup avec tes amis.

_____

6 Je _____ (*mettre*) mes bottes noires.

_____

> ⭐ If you have two names as the subject, you use the 'they' form of the verb.

> ⭐ Pay attention to the word <u>before</u> the gap so that you know which form of the verb to use.

Ⓗ 4 Write the correct irregular verb in each gap.

1 Je _____ souvent au théâtre.

2 Nous _____ un hamster et un chien.

3 _____-vous français?

4 Tu ne _____ jamais de natation.

5 Elle _____ quinze ans.

6 Mon père _____ du shopping le samedi.

> Remember that *mon père* is the same as *il*.

5 Translate these sentences into French.

1 My best friend, Sophie, does gymnastics once a week.

> *Sophie* is the same as *elle*.

_____

2 They have a big kitchen.

> The adjective has to agree.

_____

3 We are going to France with some friends. _____

Ⓗ 6 Now translate this passage into French.

> Think carefully about the word to use here.

> Think carefully about the verb here.

My brother goes to the library on Saturdays because he is very hard-working. I go horse-riding because I am sporty but my two sisters are lazy. They go out at the weekend. Do you have any brothers or sisters?

> No word for 'at' in French.

_____

_____

_____

_____

Verbs   The present tense: reflexive verbs

» Foundation pp. 12–13
» Higher pp. 12–13

(G) Reflexive verbs are common in French, and are often used to describe feelings or daily-routine activities. They have an extra part to them called a <u>reflexive pronoun</u>. You can think of this reflexive pronoun, which goes in front of the verb, as the equivalent of 'myself', 'yourself', 'himself/herself', etc. in English. The verb itself may be regular or irregular, and is conjugated in the usual way.

Reflexive verbs are important as they are frequently used in everyday language in French. For example, in English you would say 'I shower', while the French translation would be *je **me** douche*, i.e. 'I shower **myself**'.

The reflexive pronoun agrees with the subject of the verb:

se laver	to get washed
je **me** lave	I get washed
tu **te** laves	you get washed
il/elle/on **se** lave	he/she/one gets washed
nous **nous** lavons	we get washed
vous **vous** lavez	you get washed
ils/elles **se** lavent	they get washed

> ⭐ It may look odd to have *nous nous* and *vous vous*, but it is correct!

Me, te and *se* change to *m', t'* and *s'* before a vowel or silent *h*.

To make a reflexive verb negative, put **ne** <u>in front of</u> the reflexive pronoun and **pas** <u>after</u> the verb:
*Je **ne** m'ennuie **pas**.*   I don't get bored.

In the infinitive you still need the appropriate pronoun:
*Je vais **me** laver.*   I'm going to get washed.
*Il va **se** laver.*   He's going to get washed.

The reflexive pronoun can also be used to mean 'each other':
*Ils **s'**aiment.*   They love **each other**.

Some reflexive verbs are followed by a preposition:
*s'entendre **avec***   to get on with   *se fâcher **contre***   to get angry with
*se confier **à***   to confide in   *s'intéresser **à***   to be interested in
*s'occuper **de***   to look after

---

1 **Complete the sentences with the correct reflexive pronoun.**

1 Elle _____ appelle Jeanette.

2 Nous _____ ennuyons beaucoup.

3 Je _____ dispute avec mes parents.

4 Tu _____ lèves à quelle heure?

5 Vous _____ promenez à la campagne.

2 **Match up the sentence halves.**

1 Je me   a se couche de bonne heure.

2 Elle   b nous reposons après le collège.

3 Vous vous   c s'habillent pour aller au collège.

4 Nous   d disputez avec le prof.

5 Ils   e lave dans la salle de bains.

Studio GCSE French © Pearson Education Limited 2016

3 Put the verb in brackets into the correct form.

1 Les filles _____ (*s'entendre*) bien avec leurs parents.

2 Je _____ (*se lever*) vers huit heures.

3 Nous _____ (*se promener*) dans la forêt.

4 Elle _____ (*se coucher*) tard.

5 Tu _____ (*se reposer*) beaucoup.

4 Complete the sentences with the correct French verb.

1 _____ (*She looks after*) son petit frère.

2 Mon copain _____ (*is called*) Marc.

3 Marc et moi _____ (*argue*) beaucoup.

4 _____ (*They get angry*) contre leurs parents de temps en temps.

5 _____ (*You* (sg) *go to bed*) très tard.

> ⭐ If another person is mentioned as well as *moi*, you'll need to use 'we' (*nous*) and the correct form of the verb.

5 Translate these sentences into French.

1 I get on well with my aunt.

_____

2 He argues with his parents.

_____

3 We are interested in sport.

_____

> Remember that 'to be interested in' is *s'intéresser à*.

ⓗ 6 Translate this passage into French.

> No word for 'in' in French.

In the evening I look after my little brother. We relax in front of the TV but we argue sometimes. He gets on well with my dad because they often go walking in the countryside. I get on well with my mum and we don't argue.

> This is a reflexive verb in French: you argue with each other.

> Where does the *ne… pas* go?

_____

_____

_____

_____

Verbs The present tense: modal verbs

>> *Foundation pp. 54–55*
>> *Higher pp. 56–57*

(G) Modal verbs are verbs which are used together with the infinitive of another verb to talk about what people can, must or want to do. If you can use them, they allow you to vary your vocabulary and structures.

verb	meaning	je	tu	il/elle/on	nous	vous	ils/elles
pouvoir	to be able	peux	peux	peut	pouvons	pouvez	peuvent
vouloir	to want	veux	veux	veut	voulons	voulez	veulent
devoir	to have to	dois	dois	doit	devons	devez	doivent
savoir	to know (how to)	sais	sais	sait	savons	savez	savent

Modal verbs are used in the following ways:

- *pouvoir*: use it to translate the English 'can' do something:

  Je peux aller en ville.　　　　　I **can** go into town.
  Ils peuvent partir.　　　　　They **can** leave.

  Probably the most common form of *pouvoir* is 'on peut' meaning 'one/you/we can':

  On peut faire des achats en ville.　　**You can** go shopping in town.

- *vouloir*: use it to express the idea of 'want to' or 'wish to':

  Je veux passer mes vacances en France.　I **want** to spend my holidays in France.
  Elle veut jouer au foot.　　　　She **wants** to play football.

- *devoir*: use it to translate the English 'have/has to' or 'must':

  Je dois aller chez ma tante.　　I **must** go to my aunt's house.
  Nous devons rentrer tôt.　　　We **have to** return early.

- *savoir*: use it to express the idea of 'know how to':

  Je (sais) nager.　　　　　I **know how** to swim.
  Elle sait danser.　　　　She **can/knows how** to dance.

> This is often translated as 'can swim' in English, but French uses *savoir* not *pouvoir*.

In all cases, the verb which follows the modal verb in French is used in the infinitive form (ending in –er, –ir or –re). When translating into English, you also use 'to …', apart from after 'can' or 'must':

Je veux sortir.　　I want **to go out.**　　*Elle doit partir.*　　She **must leave.**

To make a modal negative, put the negative expression around the modal verb.

Je ne peux pas venir ce soir.　　I **can't** come tonight.

Like other verbs, modal verbs are used in different tenses. No matter which tense it is in, a modal verb is always followed by the infinitive.

1 Choose the correct form of the verb to complete each sentence.

1 Elle *sais / sait* jouer du piano.

2 Nous *voulons / veulent* aller au cinéma.

3 Je *peux / peut* sortir.

4 Vous *devez / doivent* rester à la maison.

5 On *peux / peut* visiter le château.

6 Nous *savons / sait* faire la cuisine.

2 Rewrite these sentences in the correct order.

1 faire ski Sais du -tu ? _____

2 doit classe en On bien travailler . _____

3 pouvons ville en Nous aller . _____

4 veut un manger Elle restaurant dans . _____

5 -vous les attendre Pouvez ? _____

6 la à voulons maison Nous rester . _____

Studio GCSE French © Pearson Education Limited 2016

3 Complete the sentences with the correct form of the verb in brackets.

1 Tu _____ (*vouloir*) faire du ski?

2 On _____ (*pouvoir*) louer un vélo.

3 Je _____ (*savoir*) parler allemand.

4 Mes copains _____ (*devoir*) rentrer avant dix heures.

5 Ils _____ (*vouloir*) passer plus de temps à la plage, mais ils _____ (*devoir*) partir.

6 Vous _____ (*devoir*) être attentifs en classe si vous _____ (*vouloir*) réussir.

> ⭐ Remember that plural nouns such as *mes copains* use the *ils* form of the verb.

4 Translate these sentences into English.

1 On peut visiter des musées intéressants. _____

2 On doit arriver à l'heure. _____

3 Ils veulent manger à la pizzeria. _____

4 Nous savons faire de la planche à voile. _____

5 Ils ne savent pas jouer de la batterie. _____

6 Nous pouvons également faire de l'escalade. _____

7 Tu dois travailler beaucoup afin de faire des progrès.

8 Elle veut manger moins de sucre car c'est mauvais pour la santé.

5 Translate these sentences into French.

1 I have to do my homework. _____

2 We want to go to Italy. _____

3 You can go horse-riding in the countryside.

> Think about which person of the verb you could use for 'you'.

Ⓗ 6 Translate this passage into French.

> Use *beaucoup à* + the infinitive here.

There's a lot to do in my town. You can watch a rugby match or you can play tennis. My friends want to go into town in the evenings but sometimes we have to do school work. Anna can speak English, so she can help the tourists.

> No word for 'in' here

> 'So' means 'therefore' here, so be careful which word you use in French.

(G) The infinitive is the form of the verb which you find in the dictionary: e.g. *jouer, finir, faire*. It is usually translated as 'to' something; e.g. 'to play', 'to finish', 'to do'. In French, all infinitives end in **–er**, **–ir** or **–re**. You will need to use the infinitive to form tenses in French. You also need to use it in a number of more complex constructions, so it is really worth knowing how and when to use the infinitive in French.

When two verbs follow each other, the second one is in the infinitive:

*J'aime **jouer**.*	I like **to play**.

Verbs followed by the infinitive

Certain verbs are followed directly by an infinitive:

- All verbs of liking, disliking and preferring such as *aimer* (to like), *adorer* (to love), *détester* (to hate) and *préférer* (to prefer):

*J'adore **regarder** la télé.*	I love **to watch** / **watching** TV.

- All modal verbs (*vouloir* (to want), *devoir* (to have to), *savoir* (to know how to), *pouvoir* (to be able to)):

*Il veut **aller** au cinéma.*	He wants **to go** to the cinema.

- Verbs expressing a future intention or wish, such as *espérer* (to hope) or *je voudrais / j'aimerais* (I'd like):

*Tu espères **aller** à l'université.*	You hope **to go** to university.

Some verbs need **à** between them and the infinitive. These include:

apprendre à	to learn to	*réussir à*	to succeed in
arriver à	to manage to	*aider à*	*to* help to
commencer à	to start to	*inviter à*	to invite to

*J'apprends à **nager**.*	I'm learning **to swim**.
*Il a réussi à **acheter** un cadeau.*	He succeeded in **buying** a present.

Some verbs need *de* between them and the infinitive. These include:

arrêter de	to stop	*oublier de*	to forget to
décider de	to decide to	*refuser de*	to refuse to
essayer de	to try to	*empêcher de*	to prevent from
continuer de	to continue to	*mériter de*	to deserve to

*J'ai oublié d'**apporter** mon livre.*	I forgot **to bring** my book.
*Nous avons décidé de **jouer** au squash.*	We decided **to play** squash.

(H) Another very useful verb to show both complexity and variety of structure is **venir de + the infinitive**. This translates the English 'to have just done something'. It is used only in two tenses:

- Use the present tense to say 'have/has just done':

*Je **viens de** partir.*	I **have just** left.
*Il **vient d'**arriver.*	He **has just** arrived.

- Use the imperfect tense to say 'had done':

*Nous **venions de** manger.*	We **had just** eaten.

(H) The infinitive is also used after *avant de* to mean 'before doing something':

Avant de partir, j'ai fermé la porte.	**Before** leaving, I closed the door.

1 **Match up the French and English sentences.**

1	J'aime chanter.	a	I hate doing my homework.
2	Je dois faire mes devoirs.	b	I try to exercise.
3	Je déteste faire mes devoirs.	c	I must do my homework.
4	J'essaie de faire de l'exercice.	d	I'm starting to play the violin.
5	Je commence à jouer du violon.	e	I like singing.

Studio GCSE French © Pearson Education Limited 2016

2 **Decide if there should be _de_, _à_ or nothing before the infinitive.**

1 Elle voudrait .... jouer au golf.

2 J'ai décidé .... faire du vélo.

3 Nous avons appris .... nager.

4 Ils n'aiment pas .... faire la vaisselle.

5 Tu essaies .... travailler plus vite.

6 Mon père a commencé .... faire de l'alpinisme.

7 Vous avez oublié .... faire vos devoirs.

8 Elle déteste .... lire.

3 **Translate the first four sentences from exercise 2 into English.**

1 ....

2 ....

3 ....

4 ....

4 **Complete the sentences with the correct infinitive (and the correct word to go in front of it, if needed).**

Example: Je voudrais aller (_to go_) à l'université.

1 Nous adorons .... (_eating_) des fruits et des légumes.

2 J'ai arrêté .... (_playing_) au rugby.

3 Vous refusez .... (_to do_) vos devoirs.

4 Elle a commencé .... (_to arrive_) à l'heure.

5 Tu as oublié .... (_to buy_) des provisions.

6 Elle veut .... (_to go_) en ville.

5 **Translate these sentences into French.**

1 I like going to Spain.

....

2 They started to play tennis.

....

3 I decided to go out.

....

Remember that some of the verbs are followed by _à_ or _de_ <u>before</u> the infinitive.

H 6 **Translate this passage into French.**

You need to use _faire_ here.

There are two words you could use for 'we'.

Last year I started to go sailing with some friends. I decided to be more active and we succeeded in learning to sail very quickly. In the future I am going to try to do windsurfing because I love doing all water sports. My brother would like to play American football.

This will be an infinitive.

You use the perfect tense to talk about the past (in French it is called the *passé composé*). It is the most commonly used past tense, so it is very important.

It is used when you are talking about single events that happened in the past: for example, 'I went', 'he ran', 'they bought'. However, it can also mean 'I have gone / I did go', 'he has run / he did run' or 'they have bought / they did buy'.

Forming the perfect tense

The perfect tense of French verbs is made up of two parts: the **auxiliary verb** + **the past participle**. The auxiliary verb must be in the present tense. Most verbs use *avoir* as the auxiliary:

j'ai	nous avons
tu as	vous avez
il/elle/on a	ils/elles ont

Then add a past participle: *J'ai **joué** au tennis.*   I **played** tennis.

Forming the past participle

To form the past participle of a regular verb:

–er verbs e.g. *manger*	remove **–er** and add **é**	mang**é**	*il a mangé* he ate
–ir verbs e.g. *finir*	remove **–r** and add **i**	fin**i**	*on a fini* we have finished
–re verbs e.g. *répondre*	remove **–re** and add **u**	répond**u**	*j'ai répondu* I answered

There are quite a lot of irregular past participles and sadly, these are the most common verbs. You will just have to learn them!

In the negative, you put **ne...pas** around the part of *avoir*:

Je n'ai pas regardé le film.   I haven't watched the film.
Elle n'a pas joué au volley.   She didn't play volleyball.

Irregular past participles

avoir ➜ eu	boire ➜ bu
être ➜ été	voir ➜ vu
dire ➜ dit	lire ➜ lu
écrire ➜ écrit	pouvoir ➜ pu
mettre ➜ mis	devoir ➜ dû
prendre ➜ pris	vouloir ➜ voulu
comprendre ➜ compris	savoir ➜ su
faire ➜ fait	

---

1   **Add the correct part of *avoir* to complete these sentences.**

Example: J'ai____ regardé la télé.

1   Ils ____ téléchargé de la musique.

2   Tu ____ préparé les légumes?

3   Elle n'____ pas fini ses devoirs.

4   Nous ____ fait du ski.

5   Vous ____ visité la France?

6   Monsieur Richard ____ perdu son passeport.

2   **Replace the infinitive in brackets with the correct past participle.**

Example: Nous avons (*acheter*) des billets.   Nous avons acheté des billets.

1   J'ai (*faire*) du vélo. ____

2   Nous avons (*manger*) un repas délicieux. ____

3   Elle a (*attendre*) le bus. ____

4   Vous avez (*voir*) le bateau. ____

5   Elles ont (*pouvoir*) acheter une voiture. ____

6   Ils ont (*écrire*) un article. ____

7   Tu as (*boire*) du café. ____

8   Les hommes ont (*finir*) leur travail. ____

3 Put the infinitive into the correct form of the perfect tense.

Samedi dernier **1** _____ (je – prendre) le car en

ville où **2** _____ (je – retrouver) ma meilleure

amie. **3** _____ (Nous – faire) les magasins et

4 _____ (elle – acheter) des baskets.

5 _____ (Nous – prendre) un burger dans un

restaurant et moi, **6** _____ (je – choisir)

un milkshake. **7** _____ (Elle – boire) un café.

8 _____ (Nous – décider) de rentrer chez moi à pied.

9 _____ (Nous – écouter) de la musique et

10 _____ (mes parents – préparer) le dîner.

> ⭐ You will need two words to form the present tense each time: a part of avoir and the past participle of the verb. There are some irregular past participles here!

4 Translate the sentences into English.

1 Elle a envoyé un e-mail. _____

2 Nous avons compris les questions. _____

3 Je n'ai pas vu le bus. _____

4 Tu as fait de la natation hier? _____

5 La semaine dernière, ils ont voulu aller au cinéma. _____

6 Vous avez joué au golf samedi dernier? _____

> ⭐ It's good practice to translate from French into English before you start to translate into French in the perfect tense. Remember that in the perfect tense there will always be a part of avoir and a past participle.

5 Translate these sentences into French.

1 She finished her homework. _____

2 We played football. _____

3 I saw the film at the cinema. _____

> Homework is plural in French.

Ⓗ 6 Now translate this passage into French.

> You could use on or nous, but remember that they use different persons of the verb.

> Use en with this form of transport.

Last year I spent my holidays at the seaside with my friends. We travelled by bus. Lionel and Joachim played tennis on the beach but Angèle read a magazine and I ate two ice creams. Later we bought some bread and some cheese and we had a picnic.

> Masculine words use du for 'some'.

As you have seen, most verbs form the perfect tense using *avoir* as the auxiliary verb, but some verbs use *être* instead. They are mostly verbs to do with movement. Some are opposites.

Forming the perfect tense

These verbs use part of the present tense of *être* + **the past participle**:

être	
je suis	nous sommes
tu es	vous êtes
il/elle/on est	ils/elles sont

English meaning	French verb	past participle
to go / to come	aller / venir	allé / venu
to arrive / to leave	arriver / partir	arrivé / parti
to go in / to go out	entrer / sortir	entré / sorti
to go up / to go down	monter / descendre	monté / descendu
to stay / to fall	rester / tomber	resté / tombé
to be born / to die	naître / mourir	né / mort
to come back	revenir	revenu
to return	retourner	retourné
to become	devenir	devenu
to go back	rentrer	rentré

⭐ DR+MRS VAN DER TRAMP spells out the first letters of the 16 verbs in the table and may help you remember them!

With these verbs, the past participle may need to change spelling as it must agree with the subject of the verb. So, for a feminine subject of a verb you would add *–e* to the end of the past participle: *elle est tombée* (she fell).

Likewise, for a masculine plural subject, add *–s*: *ils sont partis* (they left).

Add *–es* for a feminine plural subject: *elles sont parties* (they left).

je suis allé(e)	I went	nous sommes allé(e)s	we went
tu es allé(e)	you went	vous êtes allé(e)(s)	you went
il est allé	he went	ils sont allé**s**	they (m) went
elle est allé**e**	she went	elles sont allé**es**	they (f) went

---

1 Complete these sentences with the correct part of *être*.

1 Nous .... arrivés très tard.

2 Elle .... allée en ville.

3 Je .... rentré chez moi.

4 Ils .... montés.

5 Tu .... tombé dans la rue.

6 Vous .... partis à onze heures.

2 Rewrite the sentences using the correct past participle of the verb in brackets.

1 Elle est (*arriver*) vers dix heures.

_____

2 Ils sont (*rester*) à la maison.

_____

3 Il est (*sortir*) avec ses copains.

_____

4 Elle est (*partir*) tôt.

_____

5 Nous (m) sommes (*entrer*) dans le salon.

_____

6 Je (f) suis (*aller*) au cinéma.

_____

⭐ Remember that the past participle must agree with the subject of the verb.

Studio GCSE French © Pearson Education Limited 2016

3 **Replace the verb in brackets with the correct form of the perfect tense. Take care as there will always be a part of *être* and a past participle.**

1 Les garçons (*arriver*) hier. ....

2 Je (m) (*naître*) en France. ....

3 Elle (*mourir*) il y a 20 ans. ....

4 Tu (f) (*aller*) au collège. ....

5 Elles (*retourner*) en Angleterre. ....

6 Il (*partir*) avec son ami. ....

4 **Translate these sentences into English. It will help you to remember that there are two parts to every perfect tense in French.**

1 Le soir, je suis allé au stade. ....

2 Nous sommes arrivés avant midi. ....

3 Mon amie est tombée. ....

4 Mon père n'est pas venu. ....

5 Je suis sorti avec Louise. ....

6 Ils sont restés à la plage. ....

5 **Translate these sentences into French.**

Remember that 'went' will be two words in French: a part of *être* and a past participle.

1 Yesterday she went to school. ....

....

2 He arrived at the station at 6 o'clock. ....

3 We went into the house. ....

H 6 **Now translate this passage into French.**

The verb *partir* needs to be followed by *de* here.

Last week I went to the museum with my brother. We left the house at 2 o'clock and we arrived in town at 2.30. Afterwards, we went to a restaurant where we stayed on the terrace. I returned home but my brother stayed in town.

Use *rester*.

Use *rentrer* in the perfect tense here.

....

....

....

....

....

....

» *Foundation pp. 98–99*
» *Higher. p 102*

G You may sometimes want to use reflexive verbs in the past tense, so you'll need to know how to use them. Remember that reflexive verbs are common French verbs, often used to describe feelings or daily routine activities. They have an extra part to them called a **reflexive pronoun**. You can think of this reflexive pronoun as the equivalent of 'myself', 'yourself', 'himself/herself', etc. (see p. 44).

In the perfect tense, all reflexive verbs take *être*, so the past participle must <u>agree</u> with the subject of the verb. Notice that the reflexive pronoun comes <u>before</u> the part of *être*.

Reflexive verb in the present tense	English meaning
je me suis habillé(e)	I got dressed
tu t'es ennuyé(e)	you got bored
il s'est couché	he went to bed
elle s'est levée	she got up
nous nous sommes lavé(e)s	we got washed
vous vous êtes promené(e)(s)	you went for a walk
ils se sont reposés	they rested
elles se sont endormies	they fell asleep.

To make a reflexive verb negative in the perfect tense, put *ne* in front of the reflexive pronoun and *pas* after the part of *être*.

*Ils **ne** se sont **pas** disputés.*   They **didn't** argue.

⭐ The first word in each sentence has a capital letter.

1 Rewrite these perfect tense sentences in the correct order.

1 me réveillé suis Je . _____

2 parents disputés Ses se sont . _____

3 t' couché Tu es . _____

4 Louis pas ne est s'amusé . _____

5 se levés Ils sont . _____

6 nous Nous lavés sommes . _____

2 Choose the correct part of the verb to complete each sentence.

1 Ma sœur ne s'est pas *douché / douchée / douchées*.

2 Les filles se sont *couchée / couchés / couchées*.

3 Ils se sont bien *amusé / amusés / amusées*.

4 Il s'est *dépêché / dépêchée / dépêchés*.

5 Les garçons se sont *levés / levées*.

6 Nous nous sommes *ennuyé / ennuyés*.

⭐ Remember that the past participle needs to agree with the subject in the perfect tense.

Studio GCSE French © Pearson Education Limited 2016

3 **Change these reflexive verbs from the present tense to the perfect tense.**

⭐ Don't forget to make the past participle agree with the person!

Example: il se couche   il s'est couché

1 elle s'habille   ....

2 nous nous ennuyons   ....

3 ils se lavent   ....

4 je me repose   ....

5 il s'intéresse   ....

6 vous vous levez   ....

7 elles s'amusent   ....

8 je me couche   ....

4 **Translate these sentences into English.**

1 Nous nous sommes dépêchés pour aller au match de foot.

2 Pendant les vacances je me suis bien entendu avec mes sœurs.

3 Les garçons se sont souvent disputés.

4 Elle s'est reposée le soir.

5 **Translate these sentences into French.**

1 She got up early.

2 He went to bed late.

3 They (m) got dressed quickly.

Ⓗ **6** **Translate this passage into French.**

Use *de moi* here.

⭐ Remember the word order and the agreement of the past participles.

Yesterday I argued with my sister because she made fun of me. We went to bed angry, but I didn't fall asleep straightaway. I got on well with my brother and he went for a walk with me. Later his friends arrived and we had a good time.

This is an adjective and must agree with the pronoun.

Think carefully about where to position the negative.

Use the reflexive verb *s'amuser*.

(G) The imperfect is another past tense which is used to describe:

- what was happening: *Il **pleuvait**.* It **was raining**.
- what used to happen: *Je **jouais** au golf.* I **used to play** golf.
- what was ongoing when something happened:
  *Je **regardais** la télé quand il est arrivé.* I **was watching** TV when he arrived.

Formation

Take the *nous* form of the present tense of the verb, cross off the **–ons** ending, then add the following imperfect-tense endings:

faire (to do)   *nous fais~~ons~~*

subject	imperfect ending
je	–ais
tu	–ais
il/elle/on	–ait
nous	–ions
vous	–iez
ils/elles	–aient

imperfect of *faire*	English meaning
je fais**ais**	I was doing / used to do
tu fais**ais**	you were doing / used to do
il/elle/on fais**ait**	he/she/one was doing / used to do
nous fais**ions**	we were doing / used to do
vous fais**iez**	you were doing / used to do
ils/elles fais**aient**	they were doing / used to do

The good news is that all verbs except **être** are regular and follow this pattern in the imperfect tense.

Être is irregular because its *nous* part does not end in *–ons*, so to form the imperfect tense, take **ét** and simply add the imperfect tense endings as follows:

j'ét**ais**	I was	nous ét**ions**	we were
tu ét**ais**	you were	vous ét**iez**	you were
il/elle/on ét**ait**	he/she/one was	ils/elles ét**aient**	they were

⭐ Take care with verbs ending in *–ger* as the *nous* form has an extra e, so 'I was eating' would be *je mangeais*.

1 Complete the grid with the imperfect tense of *avoir*.

j' avais ✓   nous avions ✓
tu avais ✓   vous aviez ✓
il/elle/on avait ✓   ils/elles avaient ✓

2 Change the verbs in brackets into the imperfect tense and underline the other four verbs in the passage in the imperfect tense.

Quand **1** j' étais ✓ (*être*) jeune, je **2** faisais ✓ (*faire*) du judo et je jouais au foot. Mon frère regardait beaucoup la télé et mes parents écoutaient souvent la radio. **3** J' avais ✓ (*avoir*) un vélo que j'aimais beaucoup.

⭐ Look out for the imperfect tense endings on words.

(H) **3** Add the correct ending to these verbs to form the imperfect tense.

1 je jou **ais** ✓   **4** nous voul **ions** ✓   **7** elles finiss **aient** ✓
2 elle habit **ait** ✓   **5** il ét **ait** ✓   **8** vous visit **iez** ✓
3 tu fais **ais** ✓   **6** ils av **aient** ✓   **9** je nag **eais** ✓

H 4 **Write the correct form of the verb in the imperfect tense, using the same verb from the first part of the sentence.**

Example: Je jouais au foot et elle ___jouait___ au foot aussi.

1 Vous habitiez en France et ils ___habitaient___ en France aussi.

2 Nous regardions la télé et tu ___regardais___ la télé aussi.

3 Mon père était content et ma mère ___était___ contente aussi.

4 Tu dormais et je ___dormais___ aussi.

5 Je faisais du parapente et elle en ___faisait___ aussi.

6 Il allait à la pêche et j' ___allais___ à la pêche aussi.

> ⭐ Read the sentences carefully and look at the subject.

H 5 **Put the verb in brackets into the correct form of the imperfect tense.**

1 Elles ___allaient___ (aller) à la piscine.

2 Je ___mangeais___ (manger) du pain le matin.

3 Nous ___faisions___ (faire) du ski nautique.

4 Elle ___buvait___ (boire) du thé.

5 Vous ___preniez___ (prendre) une douche.

6 On ___avait___ (avoir) de la chance.

6 **Translate these sentences into English.**

1 J'attendais le bus devant ma maison. I was waiting for the bus in front of my house

2 Elle faisait de la natation à la piscine. She was swimming in the pool

3 Nous jouions au foot au centre sportif. We were playing football in the sports centre

4 Ils partaient à dix heures. they were leaving at 10 o'clock

5 Tu lisais un magazine. you were reading the magazine

6 Elles buvaient du coca. they were drinking some cola

> ⭐ Remember that the imperfect tense translates the ideas of 'was/were doing' or 'used to do'.

7 **Translate these sentences into French.**

1 I was going to town. J'allais en ville

2 He used to be an engineer. il était ingénieur

3 We were doing an apprenticeship. nous faisions un apprentissage

> Don't forget, you don't use articles with jobs in French.

> No word for 'were' here as it is part of the imperfect tense.

H 8 **Now translate this passage into French.**

Last year I was happy. I used to like school because it was interesting. My friends used to play football with me and we used to go shopping together at the weekend. My dad often used to buy presents for all the family.

> Here, 'go' is part of the verb *faire*.

> You don't need a word for 'at' here.

L'année dernière j'étais heureux j'aimais l'école car c'était interessant Mes amis jouaient au foot avec moi et le weekend nous faisions du shopping ensemble le weekend Mon père souvent achetait des cadeaux pour toute la famille

(G) The perfect and imperfect tenses have different meanings:

- Use the imperfect tense to describe what things <u>were like</u> in the past, or what <u>used to happen</u>.
- Use the perfect tense to say what somebody <u>did</u> / <u>has done</u> (a single event in the past).

However, they are often used together in the same sentence. For example, you might want to say that something **was happening** (imperfect tense), when another event <u>took place</u> (perfect tense):

Je traversais la rue quand j'ai vu mon copain.   I **was crossing** the street when <u>I saw</u> my friend.

The sentence could be turned around, but the verbs would remain in the same tense:

*<u>J'ai vu</u> mon copain quand **je traversais** la rue.*   <u>I saw</u> my friend when **I was crossing** the road.

The imperfect tense is also used for descriptions in the past, so is likely to occur in the same sentence as the perfect tense:

J'étais triste car mon équipe préférée <u>a perdu</u>.   I **was** sad because my favourite team <u>lost</u>.

---

1 **Write down which tense you would translate these phrases into.**

Example: I was happy imperfect

1   they arrived ~~prest~~ perfect
2   we used to live imperfect
3   you won perfect

4   I was swimming imperfect
5   they were tired imperfect
6   the people left perfect

---

2 **Choose the correct form of the appropriate tense in these sentences.**

1   Nous *allaient* / <u>*allions*</u> au collège quand nous *a vu* / <u>*avons vu*</u> l'accident.

2   Tu *faisais* / *faisait* du shopping quand tes copains <u>*sont partis*</u> / *sont parties*.

3   J'<u>*étais*</u> / *était* dans ma chambre quand elle <u>*est sortie*</u> / *sont sorties*.

4   Quand tu <u>*as remarqué*</u> / *a remarqué* l'incident, je *bavardait* / <u>*bavardais*</u> avec Annie.

5   Ma sœur *lisais* / <u>*lisait*</u> un magazine quand je <u>*suis arrivé*</u> / *sommes arrivés*.

6   Elles *regardait* / <u>*regardaient*</u> la télé quand il *es venu* / <u>*est venu*</u>.

> ⭐ In question 1, the first verb is in the imperfect tense as it means 'were going', but the second verb is in the perfect tense as it is a completed action in the past: 'we saw'.

> ⭐ Pay attention to detail – remember that the perfect tense always has two parts, a part of *avoir* or *être* and a past participle.

3 **Put the verb in brackets into the correct form of either the imperfect or the perfect tense.**

Example: J'allais (*aller*) en ville quand j'ai vu (*voir*) mes copains.

1   Elle était (*être*) en vacances quand elle a rencontré (*rencontrer*) un beau garçon.

2   Je faisais (*faire*) les magasins quand ma copine a téléphoné (*téléphoner*).

(H) 3   Nous jou (*jouer*) au badminton quand Marc _____ (*arriver*).

(H) 4   Ils _____ (*manger*) le dessert quand je _____ (*sonner*).

4 Translate the verbs into French using the correct tense (imperfect or perfect).

⭐ If you see 'was/were doing', you will need the imperfect tense. For the perfect tense, remember that there are always two parts.

1 I was going ....

2 he went ....

3 she was waiting ....

4 they waited ....

5 we were playing ....

6 you (sg) played ....

7 they were drinking ....

8 he drank ....

5 Translate these sentences into French. Look carefully at the tense.

1 I was going to the shops.

2 He was chatting with his friends.

3 I went to the shops.

4 He chatted to his friends.

⭐ Remember that the first verb is in the imperfect tense and the second is in the perfect tense.

6 Now translate these sentences into French.

1 We were going to school when we saw the car.

2 He was sleeping when I arrived.

3 I was finishing my homework when the telephone rang.

7 Translate this passage into French.

You need 'que' here.

It was my birthday yesterday. I was opening my cards when my aunt telephoned. She said that she was going to arrive an hour later. I was very surprised. She arrived by car and my parents were happy to see her.

For descriptions, you need the imperfect of *être* + an adjective.

Which auxiliary verb does 'arrive' take in the perfect tense?

Verbs   The near future tense

» *Foundation pp. 14–15*
» *Higher pp. 14–15*

(G) Using different tenses is a good way of showing variety and complexity in your written and spoken French. Using the near future can help with this. When you are talking about <u>what you are going to do</u> or what is <u>going to happen</u> in the future, you use the **near future tense** (*le futur proche* in French).

To form this, you need the correct part of the verb *aller* (to go) in the present tense and an infinitive. This makes it easy to translate because we also use the verb 'to go' in English.

*Je **vais** manger.*   I'm **going to** eat.
*Nous **allons** partir.*   We are **going to** leave.

Remember all the parts of *aller*:

je vais	I'm going	*nous allons*	we are going
tu vas	you are going	*vous allez*	you are going
il/elle/on va	he/she/one is going	*ils/elles vont*	they are going

Remember that the infinitive is the part of the verb you find in the dictionary and always ends in *–er*, *–ir* or *–re*: e.g. *jouer, venir, prendre*.

1 Choose the correct form of *aller* to complete the near future sentences.

1 Nous *vais / allons* regarder un film.

2 Je *vas / vais* télécharger de la musique.

3 Mon ami *vont / va* arriver en retard.

4 Tu *vas / va* partir en vacances.

5 Elles *allons / vont* voir un concert.

6 Vous *allez / allons* sortir ce soir.

⭐ The first word in the sentence has a capital letter!

2 Rewrite these near future sentences in the correct order.

1 visiter allons un Nous château . _____

2 vont leurs Elles devoirs faire . _____

3 tennis allez au jouer Vous ? _____

4 vais avec mes Je amis parler . _____

5 Les vont radio la écouter garçons . _____

6 vas finir devoirs tes Tu . _____

7 aller Elle à pêche la va . _____

8 manger Ils un dans restaurant vont . _____

3 Complete these near future sentences with the correct form of aller.

1 Vous _____ manger dans un petit restaurant en ville.

2 Je _____ jouer au squash avec mon ami.

3 Nous _____ faire du vélo.

4 Ils _____ vendre leurs ordinateurs.

5 Tu _____ acheter des provisions.

6 Elle _____ sortir bientôt.

LOCATION: 7€ PAR HEURE

Studio GCSE French © Pearson Education Limited 2016

4 Fill in the gap with an appropriate verb in the infinitive.

1 Je vais _____ du vélo.

2 Elle va _____ un sandwich.

3 Nous allons _____ la France.

4 Ils vont _____ au cinéma.

5 Translate these sentences into English.

1 Je vais faire les magasins cet après-midi.

2 Elles vont regarder un film ce soir.

3 Nous allons passer le week-end prochain à Paris.

4 Ma famille va jouer aux cartes.

6 Translate these sentences into French.

> Remember that there won't be a word for 'is', 'are' or 'am' before 'going'.

1 He is going to play football this morning.

2 We are going to visit the castle tomorrow.

3 I'm going to watch TV in my bedroom.

Ⓗ 7 Translate this passage into French.

> This needs *chez* followed by 'my friend'.

I'm going to spend the weekend at my friend's house. We are going to listen to music and chat with our friends on Skype. My brother is going to go windsurfing with my Dad and in the evening they are going to go to the ice rink. What are you going to do?

> Use *faire* not *aller* here.

> Don't forget you don't need a word for 'in' here.

Verbs The future tense

≫ *Foundation p. 139*
≫ *Higher pp. 84–85*

 In addition to using *aller* + the infinitive (the near future tense), you will also need to be able to recognise the **future tense** (and use it at Higher tier), which translates the English '**will/shall**' do something.

- You use the near future to mean the English '<u>to be going to</u>' do something.
- You use the simple future tense to express intentions.

Formation

To form the future tense of regular verbs, you need to find the **stem** and simply add the **future tense endings**. The stem is formed in one of two ways, depending on whether it is an *–er* or *–ir* verb or an *–re* verb:

future tense stem for regular verbs		future tense endings	English meaning
–er /*–ir* verbs	use the infinitive	*je jouer**ai***	I will play
–re verbs	remove the final *–e* from the infinitive	*tu jouer**as*** *il/elle/on jouer**a*** *nous jouer**ons*** *vous jouer**ez*** *ils/elles jouer**ont***	you will play he/she/one will play we will play you will play they will play

manger ➔ *je mangerai* (I shall/will eat)   *répondre* ➔ *je répondrai* (I shall/will reply)
finir ➔ *je finirai* (I shall/will finish)

Remember that there is no word for 'will/shall' in French when it is part of the future tense. In addition, we often abbreviate 'will/shall' to ''ll' in English but there is no such abbreviation in French.

Be careful: a few common verbs don't use the infinitive to form the future tense and these need to be learned separately. The good news is that all the endings remain the same.

infinitive	future tense	English meaning
aller	j'irai	I will go
avoir	j'aurai	I will have
être	je serai	I will be
faire	je ferai	I will do
devoir	je devrai	I will have to

infinitive	future tense	English meaning
pouvoir	je pourrai	I will be able to
savoir	je saurai	I will know
venir	je viendrai	I will come
voir	je verrai	I will see
vouloir	je voudrai	I will want

H Using a variety of tenses correctly shows an ability to demonstrate range and complexity of language, so it will be important to be able to use this tense in your spoken and written French at Higher tier.

1 Identify the tense of the underlined verbs: perfect (P), future (Fu) or present (Pr)?

★ Look at the verbs, note the endings and see if there is a past participle.

1 Hier <u>je suis allé</u> à la piscine. _____

2 Demain <u>il fera</u> du judo. _____

3 D'habitude <u>nous mangeons</u> vers midi. _____

4 <u>J'ai joué</u> au tennis le week-end dernier mais ce week-end <u>je visiterai</u> l'aquarium. _____ , _____

5 <u>Ils achètent</u> des cadeaux qu'<u>ils</u> leur <u>donneront</u> plus tard. _____ , _____

6 <u>Vous avez bu</u> beaucoup d'eau, alors vous <u>serez</u> en bonne santé. _____ , _____

2 Identify the tense of the verbs in this passage, then translate the passage into English.

★ Look for extra clues like time indicators.

Hier mon copain **1 a fini** ses devoirs, puis il **2 est venu** chez moi. Aujourd'hui nous **3 ferons** les magasins ensemble car il **4 veut** de nouveaux vêtements. Nous **5 fêterons** bientôt son anniversaire.

1 _____   3 _____   5 _____

2 _____   4 _____

_____

_____

Studio GCSE French © Pearson Education Limited 2016

H 3 **Add the correct ending to these future tense verbs.**

1 nous jouer _____ 3 on attendr _____ 5 je finir _____

2 ils manger _____ 4 vous partir _____ 6 tu dir _____

H 4 **Complete the sentences with the correct future tense form of the verb in brackets.**

⭐ All the verbs follow the regular pattern.

1 Vous _____ (*porter*) des baskets.

2 Je _____ (*prendre*) une douche.

3 Elles _____ (*bavarder*) beaucoup.

4 Nous _____ (*arriver*) en Espagne.

5 Tu _____ (*choisir*) une nouvelle jupe.

6 Il _____ (*inviter*) ses copains chez lui.

⭐ Remember that although the stem is irregular, the future endings remain the same.

H 5 **Now try these irregular verbs.**

1 Ils _____ (*devoir*) rentrer avant dix heures.

2 Nous _____ (*avoir*) de la chance.

3 Elles _____ (*venir*) chez nous.

4 Je _____ (*être*) riche.

5 On _____ (*aller*) au cinéma.

6 Tu _____ (*pouvoir*) sortir.

H 6 **Complete these sentences with the correct form of the future tense.**

⭐ Remember that there is no French word for 'will' here.

1 L'année prochaine _____ en France. (*we will go*)

2 _____ de Londres vers 9 heures. (*we will leave*)

3 _____ au basket. (*I will play*)

4 _____ dans une caravane. (*My parents will sleep*)

5 Demain _____ le château. (*we will visit*)

6 _____ les devoirs. (*I will do*)

⭐ You will often need to know expressions like *demain* (tomorrow), *la semaine prochaine* (next week), *le week-end prochain* (next weekend), *le mois prochain* (next month) or *l'année prochaine* (next year) when you are using the future tense.

H 7 **Translate these sentences into French.**

1 We will go out next week. _____

2 I will see my friends next month. _____

3 She will be here tomorrow. _____

H 8 **Translate this passage into French.**

Remember it is *faire du camping.*

Next year I will go to Scotland with my family. We will go camping in the north. My brother will travel by train but we will take the car. My parents say that it will be hot. I will sleep in a tent with my brother but there will be a caravan for my parents.

Use the future tense of *il y a* (there is).

_____

_____

_____

_____

G The conditional is used to say what you <u>would</u> do or what <u>would</u> happen. You use it to talk about what you would do and how things would be, for example if you were rich, or if you had more time. You probably already know *je voudrais* (I would like) but may not have realised that it was a conditional tense.

The conditional can be used for making suggestions too:

On **pourrait** aller au stade.   We **could** go to the stadium.

Forming the conditional

The conditional is formed in a similar way to the future tense, using the same stem (usually the infinitive), but adding the <u>imperfect tense</u> endings. This makes it easy to form if you know the other two tenses well.

Conditional for *aimer*	English meaning
j'aimer**ais**	I would like
tu aimer**ais**	you would like
il/elle/on aimer**ait**	he/she/one would like
nous aimer**ions**	we would like
vous aimer**iez**	you would like
ils/elles aimer**aient**	they would like

⭐ Remember that just as there was no word for 'will' in the future, there is no word for 'would' in the conditional. Similarly, although 'I would' is sometimes abbreviated to 'I'd' in English, there is no such abbreviation in French.

Verbs which are irregular in the future tense (see p. 62) are also irregular in the conditional as they keep the same stem:

aller → **ir** → *j'irais*   *faire* → **fer** → *je ferais*   *venir* → **viendr** → *je viendrais*
avoir → **aur** → *j'aurais*   *pouvoir* → **pourr** → *je pourrais*   *voir* → **verr** → *je verrais*
être → **ser** → *je serais*   *savoir* → **saur** → *je saurais*   *vouloir* → **voudr** → *je voudrais*
devoir → **devr** → *je devrais*

It is always useful to add a little variety to your French and one way of doing this is to use the conditional from time to time.

H *si*

You may see the conditional after *si* (if) in sentences with *si* + the **imperfect** + the <u>conditional</u> (see p. 84). Use this when you are talking about how things would be if something else was the case:

*Si tu **mangeais** bien, tu n'<u>aurais</u> pas faim.*   If you **ate** well, you <u>wouldn't</u> be hungry.

1 **Underline the verbs in the conditional.**

1 Elle <u>jouerait</u> au foot avec ses copains.
2 Nous <u>ferions</u> du vélo ensemble.
3 Ils <u>aimeraient</u> habiter en Espagne.
4 Tu <u>gagnerais</u> beaucoup d'argent.
5 Vous <u>visiteriez</u> les monuments historiques.
6 Il <u>serait</u> très content d'aller au Japon.

2 **Complete the sentences with the correct conditional form of *aimer* or *vouloir*.**

1 Je __voudrais__ ✓ (*vouloir*) être riche un jour.
2 Elle __aimerait__ ✓ (*aimer*) voyager.
3 Nous __voudrions__ ✓ (*vouloir*) travailler à l'étranger. (abroad)
4 Ils __aimeraient__ ✓ (*aimer*) faire du karaté.

3 **Translate this passage into English.**

J'aimerais aller en vacances en Italie avec ma famille. Nous achèterions des cadeaux et des souvenirs pour nos amis et ce serait super. Mes parents visiteraient les musées et ma sœur irait au théâtre mais je préférerais aller au bord de la mer.

I would like to go on holiday to Italy with my family. We would buy presents and souvenirs for our friends and it would be great. My parents would visit museums and my sister would go to the theater but I would prefer to go to the seaside.

Studio GCSE French © Pearson Education Limited 2016

H 4 Add the correct ending to make verbs in the conditional.

1 ils vendr _aient_ ✓   3 elle voudr _ait_ ✓   5 vous verr _iez_ ✓
2 je fer _ais_ ✓   4 tu aimer _ais_ ✓   6 nous compter _ions_ ✓

H 5 Put the verb in brackets into the conditional.

> ⭐ All the verbs are regular.

1 Ma mère _acheterait_ ✓ (*acheter*) un nouvel appartement.
2 Je _visiterais_ ✓ (*visiter*) beaucoup de pays différents.
3 Ils _vendraient_ ✓ (*vendre*) leur vieille voiture.
4 Nous _mettrions_ (*mettre*) de l'argent sur son compte bancaire.   *-RE verbs, just drop e.
5 Tu _lirais_ (*lire*) plein de romans.
6 Vous _habiteriez_ ✓ (*habiter*) une grande maison en ville.

H 6 Now put these irregular verbs into the conditional.

> ⭐ All the verbs have irregular stems but the endings remain regular.

1 Ils _seraient_ ✓ (*être*) contents.
2 Nous _ferions_ ✓ (*faire*) les magasins.
3 Vous _voudriez_ ✓ (*vouloir*) aller aux États-Unis.
4 Je _aurais_ ✓ (*avoir*) beaucoup d'amis.
5 Tu _verrais_ ✓ (*voir*) tout le monde.
6 Elle _pourrait_ ✓ (*pouvoir*) acheter une nouvelle maison.

H 7 Complete the sentences to show what these people would do if they won the lottery.

> ⭐ Remember, there is no word for 'would'. Make sure you have the correct ending, depending on the subject of the sentence.

1 Nous _irions_ ✓ (*would go*) en Amérique.
2 Ils _donneraient_ (*would give*) de l'argent à leurs amis.
3 Je _aimerais_ ✓ (*would like*) faire un tour du monde.
4 Tu _mangerais_ ✓ (*would eat*) au meilleur restaurant.
5 Elle _acheterais_ ✓ (*would buy*) une grande maison de luxe.
6 Vous _habiteriez_ ✓ (*would live*) aux États-Unis.

H 8 Translate these sentences into French.

> Remember that 'new' is an adjective which comes before the noun it describes and it is irregular.

1 I would be able to buy a new car. _Je pourrais acheter une nouv~~eau~~ voiture_ elle
2 She would visit Canada. _Elle visiterait ~~au~~ Canada._ ✓ le
3 They would invite their friends to a party. _Ils inviteraient leurs amis à une fête_

H 9 Translate this passage into French.

> beaucoup de

> Remember the position of *y* in French.

I would like to travel to Italy with my family because my uncle lives there. We would go shopping in Milan and I would buy lots of new clothes. My brothers would watch a football match and my mum and I would sunbathe because it would be sunny.

> What verb do you usually use with the weather?

> You will need the *nous* form of the verb here.

J'aimerais voyager en Italie ✓ avec ma famille parce que
mon oncle habite y. Nous ~~ferions~~ du shopping à   là
Milan et j'achèterais beaucoup de vêtements. Mes frères   nouveux
regarderaient un match de foot et ma mère et moi ~~bronze~~   bronzerions
parce qu'il y aurais du soleil

or il serait ensoleillé

» *Foundation p. 75*
» *Higher pp. 76–77*

G You need to use the imperative when you want to tell someone to <u>do</u> something, give instructions, make a request, express a wish, offer advice or recommend something: 'Eat this!', 'Sit down!', 'Let's go!'.

In French, there are three forms of the imperative:

- You use the **tu** form with a person you know or if you are being friendly:
  Finis *tes devoirs!*   Finish your homework!

- The **vous** form is used for more than one person, for people you don't know or if you are being polite:
  Finissez *vos devoirs!*   Finish your homework!

- The **nous** form means '*let's…*':
  Finissons *nos devoirs!*   Let's finish our homework!

For all regular and most irregular –ir and –re verbs, the imperative is simply formed by dropping the subject pronoun (*tu*, *vous*, *nous*) from the appropriate form of the present tense:

~~Tu~~ **Vends!** Sell!   ~~Vous~~ **Vendez!** Sell!   ~~Nous~~ **Vendons!** Let's sell!

The rules for –er verbs are the same, except the final *s* is dropped from the *tu* form:

Manges! Eat!   **Regardes!** Watch!

Aller follows the same pattern, so the *tu* command form is *va*. *Ouvrir* does the same, despite not being an –er verb:

Ouvre! Open!

H There are three irregular imperatives:

	avoir (to have)	être (to be)	savoir (to know)
tu	aie	sois	sache
nous	ayons	soyons	sachons
vous	ayez	soyez	sachez

The imperative of reflexive verbs is different: Add the pronoun *–toi*, *–nous* or *–vous* to the command and separate it with a hyphen:

s'asseoir: *Assieds-toi!* Sit down!   *Asseyons-nous!* Let's sit down!   *Asseyez-vous!* Sit down!

1 Fill in the gaps in this table.

infinitive	*tu* form imperative	*nous* form imperative	*vous* form imperative
aller	vas ✗	allons ✓	allez
faire	fais	faisons ✓	faites ✓
manger	manges ✗	mangeons	mangez ✓
répondre ✓	répondes ✓	répondons	répondez

2 Match up the French and English sentences.

1 Ouvrez la porte!   a Close the door! ✓

2 Vas chez toi!   b Watch the TV! ✓

3 Ferme la porte!   c Open the door! ✓

4 Écoutons de la musique!   d Go to your house! ✓

5 Regarde la télé!   e Let's listen to some music! ✓

Studio GCSE French © Pearson Education Limited 2016

3 Put the verb in brackets into the correct form of the imperative.

1 _mangeons_ (manger – nous) ensemble!

2 _viens venez_ (venir – vous) au stade!

3 _bois_ (boire – tu) du coca!

4 _allons_ (aller – nous) au café!

5 _tournez_ (tourner – vous) à gauche!

6 _~~traveres~~ traverses_ (traverser – tu) la rue!

4 Translate these sentences into English.

1 N'oubliez pas de changer de trains!

Don't forget to change trains.

2 Entrez tout de suite!

enter right now

3 Visitez notre ville!

Visit our city

4 Fais une activité sportive!

do a sports activity

5 Translate these commands into French.

1 Do your homework! (*tu*)

faistes devoirs

> Remember that you don't need to include the word for 'you' in the imperative.

2 Arrive at school on time! (*vous*)

Arrivez à l'école à temps. _à l'heure_

> How would you say 'on time' in French?

3 Let's go to the train station!

allons à la gare

H 6 Translate this passage into French.

> Which imperative form do you need here?

> You could use the *tu* or *vous* imperative form in this passage, or a mixture of both for practice.

Let's go to the theatre! Take the bus and get off at the town hall. Cross the square and turn left. Continue straight on until the traffic lights. The theatre is on the right. Go in, buy a ticket, sit down and drink a coffee!

> Use the Imperative form of *descendre*.

> Use the imperative form of *entrer*.

> Remember to add the reflexive pronoun in the correct position.

Allons à la au théâthe! Prenez le bus et descendez à la mairie. Traversez la place et tournez à gauche. Continuez tout droit jusqu'aux feux. de signalisation Le théâthe se trouve est à droite à droite. Entrez achetez un ticket billet, asseyez -vous et buvez un café.

>> *Foundation pp. 160–161*
>> *Higher pp. 110–111*

 The pluperfect tense is another past tense, but it is not used as frequently as the perfect and imperfect tenses. It is used to say what you <u>had</u> done, so you'll see it when talking about an event which took place one step further back than another past event or what <u>had</u> happened in the past:

J'avais déjà mangé quand il est arrivé. I **had** already **eaten** when he arrived.

Forming the pluperfect tense

Like the perfect tense, the pluperfect is formed of two parts: an auxiliary verb (*avoir* or *être*) + the past participle. The difference is that it uses the <u>imperfect tense</u> of the auxiliary verb:

J'avais fini. I **had** finished. *Elle était partie.* She **had** arrived.

> ⭐ Remember that the English abbreviation of 'I had' to 'I'd', etc. does not occur in French.

The same verbs take *être* in the pluperfect tense as in the perfect tense: see pp. 52–53, and remember DR + MRS VAN DER TRAMP. Remember too that with verbs which take *être*, the past participle of the verb must agree with the subject:

Ils étaient arrivés. They had arrived.

The pluperfect with *avoir*

pluperfect of *manger*	English meaning
j'**avais** mangé	I had eaten
tu **avais** mangé	you had eaten
il/elle/on **avait** mangé	he/she/one had eaten
nous **avions** mangé	we had eaten
vous **aviez** mangé	you had eaten
ils/elles **avaient** mangé	they had eaten

The pluperfect with *être*

pluperfect of *aller*	English meaning
j'**étais** allé(e)	I had gone
tu **étais** allé(e)	you had gone
il/elle/on **était** allé(e)(s)	he/she/it had gone
nous **étions** allé(e)s	we had gone
vous **étiez** allé(e)(s)	you had gone
ils/elles **étaient** allé(e)s	they had gone

To make the pluperfect tense negative, put *ne…pas* around the part of *avoir* or être, just as in the perfect tense.

1 Decide which sentences contain a verb in the perfect tense (P) and which ones contain a verb in the pluperfect tense (PP).

1 J'avais fini mon petit-déjeuner. _____
2 Nous avons mangé de la viande. _____
3 Elle est arrivée au stade. _____
4 Ils avaient demandé de l'argent. _____
5 Tu as fait du camping. _____
6 Elles étaient allées en Allemagne. _____
7 Vous aviez fait vos devoirs. _____
8 Il a rangé sa chambre. _____

2 Match up the French and English sentences.

1 Elle est rentrée chez elle.
2 Nous avions visité la tour.
3 On a regardé un film.
4 Ils étaient allés au centre sportif.
5 J'ai joué au hockey.
6 Tu avais oublié tes affaires.

a You had forgotten your things.
b They had gone to the leisure centre.
c She returned home.
d I played hockey.
e We had visited the tower.
f We watched a film.

3 Translate these sentences into English.

1 Tu avais déjà fini ton déjeuner. _____
2 Elle n'avait jamais lu ce livre. _____
3 Ils étaient allés au Maroc. _____
4 Elle était venue toute seule. _____

3 **Make the following sentences negative using the negative in brackets.**

> Remember that *du*, *de la*, *de l'* and *des* all change to *de* or *d'* after a negative. Remember too that *ne* must change to *n'* before a vowel or silent *h*.

1 Je mange de la viande. (*ne...jamais*) _____

2 Elle va au cinéma. (*ne...pas*) _____

3 Tu aimes les documentaires. (*ne...plus*) _____

4 Il a dix euros. (*ne...que*) _____

5 Elles aiment le cyclisme. (*ne...pas*) _____

6 J'adore les maths et le français. (*ne...ni...ni*) _____

> *J'* will need to change to *Je* when you use the negative.

4 **Translate these sentences into English. Take care with the negatives.**

1 Nous n'aimons ni la géo ni l'histoire. _____

2 Elle n'est jamais allée en Allemagne. _____

3 Vous n'avez rien fait. _____

4 Je ne vais pas faire de vélo ce soir. _____

5 **Translate these sentences into French.**

> 'Living' will be an infinitive in French.

1 We don't like living in town.

_____

2 She isn't going to the castle.

_____

3 They have never played football.

_____

H **6** **Translate this passage into French.**

> *C'* in *c'était* will change to *ce n'* in the negative.

I don't like maths any more. The teacher is never happy and we do not do anything. Last year it was never boring. Nobody works in class. Yesterday he didn't explain the questions and I didn't know what to do.

> Remember, *personne* must be followed by *ne*.

> Use *quoi* for 'what' here.

_____

_____

_____

_____

(G) Impersonal verbs are only used with *il*. They are quite common in French, so you will need to know them. You will know some already such as *il y a* (there is/are) and words associated with the weather: *il pleut* (it's raining), *il neige* (it's snowing), etc.

The most common impersonal verb is *il faut*, which can be translated as 'it is necessary to'. This sometimes sounds rather clumsy in English, so we tend to use 'you must' or 'you have to', but it can have other meanings too.

Il faut is followed by the infinitive. You might also use it in the negative: put *ne…pas* around *faut* to give *il ne faut pas*:

Il faut manger des légumes.	**You must** eat vegetables.
Il faut travailler pour réussir.	**It's necessary** to work in order to succeed.
Il ne faut pas boire trop de café.	**You must not** drink too much coffee.

Other common impersonal verbs include *il est interdit de* + infinitive (it's forbidden to / you mustn't):

Il est interdit de fumer.	**You mustn't** smoke. / Smoking **is forbidden**.

(H) Other uses of *il faut* include:

Il me faut du beurre.	I need some butter.
Il faut une heure pour y aller en voiture.	It takes an hour to get there by car.

Some impersonal constructions like *il faut* may be followed by *que* + the subjunctive, but don't worry, you will only need to recognise them:

Il faut que je travaille.	I must work.

1 **Write these sentences in the correct order.**

1 faut Il heure arriver à l'.

_____

2 ne faut Il en classe manger pas.

_____

3 ses Il devoirs faut faire.

_____

4 Il attentif être faut classe en.

_____

5 porter bijoux ne faut Il de pas.

_____

2 **Match up the English and French sentences.**

1	Il est interdit de fumer.	**a**	You must not drink alcohol.
2	Il faut rester au lit.	**b**	Smoking is forbidden.
3	Il ne faut pas boire d'alcool.	**c**	You must take a ticket.
4	Il est interdit de jouer au foot.	**d**	You must stay in bed.
5	Il faut prendre un ticket.	**e**	Playing football is banned.

3 **Complete the sentences with a word from the box. (There are more words than you need!)**

1 Il faut _____ attentif.

2 Il est _____ de marcher sur la pelouse.

3 Il ne _____ pas fumer.

4 Il est interdit d'_____ en ville en voiture.

5 Il ne faut _____ consommer trop de sucre.

aller	manger	est	être
pas	a	faut	interdit

⭐ Make sure that what you have added makes sense.

4 **Translate these sentences into English.**

⭐ Make sure what you have written makes sense in English and sounds natural.

1 Il faut avoir un parapluie quand il pleut.

2 Il est interdit de fumer dans les restaurants.

3 Il ne faut pas manger trop de fast-food.

4 Il est interdit de laisser tomber des papiers dans la rue.

5 **Translate these sentences into French.**

⭐ Each sentence will contain an infinitive.

1 You mustn't speak in class.

2 You must study English and maths.

3 Wearing jewellery is not permitted.

H 6 **Translate this passage into French.**

Remember, these will be infinitives.

There are lots of rules in my school in France. You must arrive before 8 o'clock. You must buy your own text books. Chewing gum is forbidden. Using mobiles in the classroom is banned. You must do homework for two hours per evening.

Start the sentence with 'it is forbidden/banned' and follow it with an infinitive.

Verbs   The present participle

» *Foundation pp. 156–157*
» *Higher p. 105*

(G) The English present participle ends in '–ing' and is used frequently. The French present participle ends in **–ant** and is far less common.

You will often see the present participle used after the word **en** to mean <u>while doing</u>, <u>in doing</u>, <u>on doing</u>: or <u>by doing</u> something:

*Il travaille **en écoutant** de la musique.*   He works **while listening** to music.
***En travaillant**, on gagne de l'argent.*   **By working**, you earn money.

Forming the present participle

To form the present participle, take **–ons** off the *nous* part of the present tense of the verb and simply add **–ant**:

travailler ➜ *travail**lons*** ➜ *travaill**ant*** (working)   *aller* ➜ *al**lons*** ➜ *all**ant*** (going)

There are three exceptions which are irregular:

avoir ➜ *ayant* (having)   *être* ➜ *étant* (being)   *savoir* ➜ *sachant* (knowing)

(H) **When to use the present participle**

Even though the present participle isn't common, it will be impressive if you know when and how to use it and also when <u>not</u> to use it. **Don't** use a present participle:

- when talking about what someone is doing in the present: 'he is working' is <u>not</u> *il est travaillant* but just the present tense, *il travaille.*
- after another verb: 'we like singing' is not *nous aimons chantant* but *nous aimons chanter*; in cases like this, an infinitive is used ('we like to sing').
- when English uses a present participle as a noun: 'playing rugby is great'; in this case an infinitive is used, so this would be *jouer au rugby (c')est super.*

The present participle does not usually change its spelling, but for reflexive verbs, you still need to use the appropriate reflexive pronoun: *en **me** couchant, en **se** couchant*, etc.

1 **Match up the French and English phrases.**

1 en faisant du camping   a on arriving at my friend's house
2 en arrivant chez mon copain   b by working hard
3 en jouant au rugby   c by going camping
4 en allant à l'étranger   d whilst playing rugby
5 en travaillant dur   e by going abroad

2 **Tick the four sentences which contain a present participle.**

1 En faisant mon travail, je vais faire des progrès. ☐
2 Nous aimons jouer du saxophone parce que c'est amusant. ☐
3 Il déteste manger des légumes car leur goût est désagréable. ☐
4 En arrivant à la maison, j'ai rencontré mon copain. ☐
5 Elle s'est cassée la jambe en jouant au foot. ☐
6 Vous avez bu deux bouteilles de coca et c'est mauvais pour les dents. ☐
7 Elles aiment faire de l'équitation. ☐
8 Tu as réussi en travaillant dur. ☐

> ★ Remember that you take the *nous* form of the present tense, cross off *–ons* and add *–ant*, so all your answers will end in *–ant*.

(H) **3** **Write the present participle of these verbs.**

1 aller ....

2 jouer ....   5 lire ....   8 finir ....

3 répondre ....   6 mettre ....   9 attendre ....

4 faire ....   7 venir ....   10 rougir ....

Studio GCSE French © Pearson Education Limited 2016

4 Translate these sentences into English. They all contain a present participle.

1 En quittant le collège, elle a rencontré sa sœur.

....

2 En rangeant ma chambre, j'ai gagné de l'argent de poche.

....

> *Gagner* has many translations in English. Which one are you going to use here?

3 En faisant la vaisselle, j'ai chanté.

....

4 En traversant la rue, ils ont vu un chien énorme.

....

H 5 Complete these sentences with the correct present participle and then translate them.

1 En .... (*manger*) du pain grillé, j'écoute la radio.

....

> ⭐ Remember that the present tense *nous* form of verbs like *nager* retains the *e*: nage*ons*.

2 En .... (*regarder*) la télé, elle m'a téléphoné.

....

3 En .... (*arriver*), nous n'avons vu personne à la réception de l'hôtel.

....

4 En .... (*partir*), j'ai commencé à rire.

....

H 6 Decide whether or not a present participle is needed or not needed in these cases. Write 'yes' or 'no'.

1 She is sleeping. ....

2 I love skateboarding. ....

3 By sending emails, we can keep in touch. ....

4 While listening to the radio, I wrote a letter. ....

H 7 Translate these sentences into French.

1 She had lunch whilst listening to the radio.

....

> ⭐ In every sentence there will be a present participle ending in –*ant*.

2 I earn money by working at the supermarket.

....

> You could use *régional* for 'local'.

3 They ate some local food whilst travelling abroad.

....

H 8 Translate this passage into French.

> Use the correct form of *accueillir*. Where will 'us' go?

> ne … personne

While visiting Paris, we ate at a restaurant. On arriving, we realised that there was no one to welcome us. While eating, we found the atmosphere really noisy and on looking at the bill, we had a shock. Eating at a restaurant is very expensive!

> Use the correct form of *regarder*.

> Remember when not to use the present participle.

....

....

....

....

>> *Higher p. 146*

G **H** The perfect infinitive is a great way of impressing your teacher and in your exam, as it enables you not only to link your ideas, but also to show off your knowledge of French grammar.

Forming the perfect infinitive

The perfect infinitive is used to translate the English 'after having done / doing' something.
You use *après* + **the infinitive of** *avoir* **or** *être* + the **past participle of the verb**. The same verbs which take *être* in the perfect tense will take *être* to form the perfect infinitive.

Après avoir joué au foot…	**After having played** football…
Après être arrivé…	**After arriving**…

All the usual rules concerning the perfect tense apply, so with verbs which use *être* the past participle must agree with the subject of the verb. This is a little more tricky in the perfect infinitive, as the <u>subject</u> of the main verb will probably come after the perfect infinitive:

*Après être **arrivés**, <u>les garçons</u> ont joué au foot.*	After **arriving**, <u>the boys</u> played football.

Here, the subject of the verbs 'to arrive' and 'to play' is *les garçons* (masculine plural), so *arrivé**s*** has the extra **s**.

The perfect infinitive of a reflexive verb needs the appropriate reflexive pronoun and follows the usual rules for verbs which take *être*:

*Après **m**'être levé**e**, j'ai pris le petit-déjeuner.*	After getting up, I had breakfast.

The subject is a girl here, so the past participle needs to agree.

The perfect infinitive of verbs which use *avoir* is easier to form, as there is no agreement:

*Après avoir **mangé**, ils ont joué au foot.*	After having eaten, they played football.

Avant de + infinitive

We've just looked at how to say '<u>after having done something</u>'. It is also useful to know how to say '<u>before doing something</u>.' To do this, you use the structure ***avant de*** + **infinitive**, e.g. *avant d'arriver* (before arriving), *avant de manger* (before eating). This can be helpful in creating more complex sentences:

Avant de partir, ils ont pris un repas au restaurant.	**Before leaving**, they had a meal at the restaurant.

H 1 **Write the perfect infinitive of these verbs.**

1 tomber _____

2 travailler _____

3 mettre _____

4 aller _____

5 faire _____

6 vendre _____

H 2 **Complete the sentences with a word from the box.**

> levés   jouer   être   mangé   avant

1 Avant de _____ au volley, elles ont déjeuné.

2 Après avoir _____ un sandwich, elle est partie.

3 Nous allons faire du vélo, après _____ arrivés.

4 J'ai nagé dans la mer _____ de bronzer.

5 Ils ont écouté de la musique après s'être _____

⭐ Remember: DR + MRS VAN DER TRAMP.

Studio GCSE French © Pearson Education Limited 2016

H 3 **Complete the sentences, using the perfect infinitive of the verb in brackets.**

1 Ils ont joué au hockey, après _____ (*aller*) au stade.

2 Nous sommes arrivés chez elle, après _____ (*prendre*) le bus.

3 Après _____ (*faire*) du judo, elle voudrait aller en ville.

4 Après _____ (*sortir*), elle a rencontré son copain.

5 Après _____ (*manger*), je vais quitter la maison.

6 J'ai joué au foot après _____ (*finir*) mes devoirs.

> ⭐ Remember to watch out for agreements with verbs which take *être*.

H 4 **Translate these sentences into English.**

1 Elle a promené le chien après s'être habillée. _____

2 Il a lu un livre après être arrivé au collège. _____

3 Nous avons mangé avant de quitter la maison.

_____

_____

4 Avant de continuer mes études, je vais passer mes examens.

_____

_____

H 5 **Translate these sentences into French.**

1 After having left school, my sister found a job.

_____

> Use the correct form of *quitter* here.

2 After finishing my exams, I hope to do an apprenticeship.

_____

3 After going to university, she would like to work in a school.

_____

_____

> Notice that the subject of the sentence is 'she', so check your perfect infinitive carefully.

H 6 **Translate this passage into French.**

> Use a form of *quitter*.

After finishing my exams, I intend to study English at university. After leaving university, I would like to travel and see different cultures. After returning home, I hope to do some voluntary work before getting married and having a family.

> Remember, this comes after 'cultures' and so has to agree with the noun.

> *avant de* + infinitive

> 'To get married' is reflexive in French.

_____

_____

_____

_____

_____

Verbs   The passive voice

» Foundation pp. 158–159
» Higher pp. 166–167

G The passive voice: present tense

The passive voice is used to talk about things that <u>are done</u> (to someone or something). It is used frequently in English but is less common in French. It is formed using a part of *être* and a past participle.

Il lit le livre.	He reads the book. (active)
but	
*Le livre **est lu**.*	The book **is read**. (passive)
Je regarde la télé (active).	I watch TV.
but	
*La télé **est regardée**.*	The TV **is watched**. (passive)

The past participle must agree with the subject. Be careful not to confuse the passive with ordinary perfect tense verbs which take *être*!

H The passive voice: other tenses

The passive voice can be used in different tenses – the only verb which changes is *être* – but the past participle remains the same.

- **Perfect:**   *Il **a été** invité.*   He **has been** invited.
- **Imperfect:** *La maison **était** enfin construite.*   The house **was** finally built.
- **Future:**   *L'appartement **sera** vendu.*   The flat **will be** sold.

A good way to avoid using the passive voice when you are speaking or writing in French is to turn the sentence round by using *on*.

   ***On** m'a invité.*   I was invited. (Literally: Someone invited me.)

---

1 Choose the correct form of *être* to complete the sentences in the passive.

1 Les fruits *est / sont* achetés.

2 La chambre *est / a* rangée.

3 La voiture *est / sont* vendue.

4 Les murs *est / sont* décorés.

5 Les clefs *est / sont* perdues.

> ⭐ Look at the past participle for help with singular and plural verbs.

2 Match up the French and English sentences.

1 Les monuments sont visités par les touristes.

2 Les portables sont vendus sur Internet.

3 Mon ordinateur est souvent utilisé.

4 La musique est téléchargée.

5 Mes devoirs sont finis.

a My computer is often used.

b Music is downloaded.

c Mobiles are sold on the internet.

d My homework is finished.

e The monuments are visited by tourists.

3 Replace the verb in brackets with the correct past participle.

1 La ville est souvent _____ (*visiter*).

2 L'espagnol est _____ (*parler*) ici.

3 Mes affaires sont souvent _____ (*perdre*).

4 Mon travail scolaire est bientôt _____ (*finir*).

5 Les animaux sauvages sont souvent _____ (*tuer*) par les chasseurs.

> ⭐ Remember that the past participle must agree with the noun.

Studio GCSE French © Pearson Education Limited 2016

H 4 Rewrite the sentences in the passive.

> Remember that when it is passive, the past participle is an adjective and must agree with the subject.

Example: Elle a cassé la porte. La porte est cassée.

1 J'ai fini le travail. _____

2 Elle a acheté les portables. _____

> This is masculine plural.

3 Nous avons mangé la pomme. _____

4 Ils ont vendu les chocolats. _____

5 Tu as bu le vin. _____

> *Fenêtres* is feminine plural.

6 Elles ont cassé les fenêtres. _____

H 5 Match up the French and English sentences.

1 Je serai attendu devant la gare.

2 Chaque fois, nous étions accueillis par tout le personnel.

3 Les cadeaux ont été reçus.

4 Mon équipe a été battue.

5 Les devoirs ont été rapidement finis.

a The homework has been finished quickly.

b The presents have been received.

c I will be waited for in front of the station.

d My team has been beaten.

e Each time, we were welcomed by all the staff.

H 6 Translate these sentences into French.

1 The window is broken.

_____

2 Lots of emails are sent every day.

_____

3 The computer is repaired.

_____

> Don't forget past participle agreement.

H 7 Translate these sentences into French.

1 More than a thousand songs are downloaded from the Internet every minute.

_____

> Don't translate 'a'.

2 I am often invited to birthday parties by my friends.

_____

> Remember, in French you say 'parties of birthday' and 'presents of birthday'.

3 All the birthday presents are bought.

_____

4 Many houses are built in France every week.

_____

> Remember that 'houses' is feminine plural.

G Some common expressions use the 'mood' of the verb called the subjunctive. You need to be able to understand the meaning of these expressions and recognise the verb forms.

H The subjunctive is used to express <u>wishes</u>, <u>thoughts</u>, <u>possibility</u> or <u>necessity</u>. It is often used after a verb which is followed by *que*:

*Je veux **que tu arrives** à l'heure.*   I want you to arrive on time.

The subjunctive mood is not a different tense, but is used instead of the indicative mood (all the tenses you have already seen) in certain circumstances.

Forming the subjunctive

For all regular verbs ending in *–er*, *–ir* and *–re*, as well as some irregular verbs, take the third person plural (*ils*) form of the present tense, cross off *–ent* and add the subjunctive endings:

Forming the stem of *parler*: *ils parlent* → *parl*

	subjunctive ending	**parler**	**choisir**	**vendre**	**partir**	**sortir**	**mettre**
je	–e	parl**e**	choisiss**e**	vend**e**	part**e**	sort**e**	mett**e**
tu	–es	parl**es**	choisiss**es**	vend**es**	part**es**	sort**es**	mett**es**
il/elle/on	–e	parl**e**	choisiss**e**	vend**e**	part**e**	sort**e**	mett**e**
nous	–ions	parl**ions**	choisiss**ions**	vend**ions**	part**ions**	sort**ions**	mett**ions**
vous	–iez	parl**iez**	choisiss**iez**	vend**iez**	part**iez**	sort**iez**	mett**iez**
ils/elles	–ent	parl**ent**	choisiss**ent**	vend**ent**	part**ent**	sort**ent**	mett**ent**

Some verbs change the stem in the *nous* and *vous* forms:

boire → *nous **buv**ions, vous **buv**iez*   *prendre* → *nous **pren**ions, vous **pren**iez*
envoyer → *nous **envoy**ions, vous **envoy**iez*   *venir* → *nous **ven**ions, vous **ven**iez*

The stem of some verbs is irregular in the present subjunctive, but the endings are the same:

faire → *je **fasse***   *pouvoir* → *je **puisse***
aller → *j'**aille***   *savoir* → *je **sache***

Vouloir has the subjunctive *je **veuille***, but also changes stem in the *nous* and *vous* forms to *nous **voul**ions* and *vous **voul**iez*.

Avoir and *être* are totally irregular:

avoir		*être*	
j'aie	nous ayons	je sois	nous soyons
tu aies	vous ayez	tu sois	vous soyez
il/elle/on ait	ils/elles aient	il/elle/on soit	ils/elles soient

Using the subjunctive

The subjunctive is used after the following expressions:

- **à condition que**   provided that
  *À condition que je **travaille** bien…*   Provided that I work well…

- **bien que**   although
  *Bien qu'il **soit** heureux…*   Although he is happy…

- **il faut que**   you/I/one must / it is necessary that
  *Il faut que j'y **aille**.*   I must go.

- **avant que**   before
  *Avant qu'elle **parte**…*   Before she leaves…

- **c'est dommage que**   it's a shame that
  C'est dommage qu'elle ne soit pas ici.   It's a shame that she isn't here.

- **pour que**   so that
  Pour que tu comprennes…   So that you understand…

- **jusqu'à ce que**   until
  *Je reste ici jusqu'à ce qu'elle **finisse**.*   I'm staying here until she finishes.

H 1 **Tick the sentences which are in the subjunctive.**

1   Avant de partir, elles ont fait leurs devoirs.   ✓
2   Elle veut que je l'accompagne.   ☑ ✓
3   Nous avons travaillé dur en classe.   ☐ ✓
4   Il faut que j'aille en ville.   ☑ ✓
5   On doit boire plus d'eau.   ☑ ✓
6   Nous allons souvent au théâtre.   ☐ ✓

H 2 **Underline the verbs in the subjunctive in this passage.**

Avant d'aller en ville, Bernard range toujours sa chambre pour qu'il puisse inviter ses amis chez lui plus tard. Il veut que ses amis s'amusent bien, alors il télécharge de la musique avant qu'ils arrivent. Ils sont très contents à condition que Bernard prépare des snacks pour eux.

H 3 **Translate these sentences into English.**

1   Bien qu'il travaille bien, il n'a pas de bonnes notes.

Although he works well, he doesn't have good grades

2   Il faut que j'aille en ville.

I have to go to town

3   Ma mère m'a offert cinquante euros à condition que je sois sage.

my mum offered me 50 euros provided that I am wise

H 4 **Translate these sentences into French.**

1   Although I live in Spain, I cannot speak Spanish.

Bien que j'habite en Espagne, je ne peux pas parler espagnol   sois

> For 'people', use _on_.

2   They want people to save electricity.

Ils veulent que on économise l'éctricité

> Use _il est possible que._

3   It might be sunny today.

il est possible que soit ensoleillé aujord'hui   il y ait du soleil
+ qu'il soit ensoleille

G You use *depuis* to translate 'for' and 'since' in French. In English we use the past tense before both of these words, but this is not always the case in French. So, if you can master the use of *depuis*, you really will be able to impress in your exams!

Depuis + present tense

To say how long you've been doing something, use the present tense with **depuis**, even though it will be translated in the past in English.

> *J'habite à Paris **depuis** trois ans.*   I've been living in Paris for three years. (and I am still living there)

However, if you just want to say <u>how long</u> you did something for in the past, you don't use *depuis* but you still use a past tense:

> *J'ai habité à Paris pendant un an.*   **I lived** in Paris for a year. (but I don't still live there)

Even when *depuis* means 'since', you still use the present tense:

> *J'habite ici **depuis** ma naissance.*   **I've been living** here **since** I was born.

H *Depuis* **+ imperfect tense**

At higher tier, you'll need to be aware of how to use **depuis** with the imperfect tense.

To say how long you <u>had</u> been doing something, use the imperfect tense with *depuis*:

> *Elle **attendait depuis** une heure.*   She **had been waiting for** an hour.

1 **Unjumble these words to make correct sentences.**

1 mal à gorge la hier depuis J'ai.

   _____

2 habite maison depuis mois Paul six sa.

   _____

3 apprenons français le depuis ans cinq Nous.

   _____

4 fait magasins depuis Elle les heures deux.

   _____

5 en au Portugal Elle vacances va deux ans depuis.

   _____

6 Nous sur depuis heures cinq jouons l'ordinateur.

   _____

2 **Choose the correct form of the verb to complete the sentences.**

1 Il *habite / a habité* à Lyon depuis sa naissance.

2 Nous *regardons / avons regardé* la télé depuis une heure.

3 *J'ai été / Je suis* ici depuis vingt minutes.

4 Elles *ont habité / habitent* leur appartement depuis cinq ans.

5 Tu *fais / as fait* du vélo depuis trente minutes.

3 **Write the correct form of the verb in the tense indicated.**

1 Vous _____ (*habiter* – present) ici depuis combien de temps?

2 Je _____ (*être* – present) ici depuis cinq minutes.

3 Il _____ (*faire* – present) du judo depuis un an.

H 4 Nous _____ (*attendre* – imperfect) à l'arrêt depuis une heure.

H 5 Elles _____ (*apprendre* – imperfect) l'anglais depuis dix ans.

> ⭐ Remember the imperfect endings:
> *je –ais*
> *tu –ais*
> *il/elle/on –ait*
> *nous –ions*
> *vous –iez*
> *ils/elles –aient*

Studio GCSE French © Pearson Education Limited 2016

4 **Fill in the gaps by translating the English words into French.**

> In each sentence you will need to use *depuis* + a period of time.

1 Elle y habite _____ (*for a year*).

2 Elle travaille dans une usine _____ (*for six months*).

3 Nous allons en vacances en Suisse _____ (*for three years*).

4 Tu fais du ski _____ (*for an hour*).

5 Elles écoutent de la musique _____ (*for 20 minutes*).

6 Vous jouez au foot _____ (*for 45 minutes*).

H 7 On regardait la télé _____ (*for half an hour*).

H 8 J'étudiais à l'université _____
   (*for four years*).

5 **Translate these sentences into French.**

> • If you want to say for how long you have or one has been doing something, use the present tense with *depuis*.
> • Remember that you won't need a word for 'been'.

1 He has been living in France for two years.

   _____

2 We have been playing rugby for ten minutes.

   _____

3 I have been dancing for thirty minutes.

   _____

4 The boys have been doing their homework for quarter of an hour.

   _____

H **6** **Now translate this passage into French.**

> Which word for 'his' do you need here? Think about the French for 'friend'.

He has been playing on the computer for two hours and his friend has been reading for twenty minutes.
His parents had been watching a film in the living room for an hour and his dog had been sleeping in the
garden for fifteen minutes.

> Think carefully about the tense you need here.

_____

_____

_____

_____

_____

Verbs   Using *si* in complex sentences

Higher pp. 106–107, p. 151

G
H Using *si* (if) clauses can demonstrate higher-level skills, as it shows that you know and understand the sequence of tenses which follow *si*:

- *si* + the present + **the future**:   *Si je travaille bien, je réussirai.*   If I work well, I **will succeed.**

- *si* + the imperfect + **the conditional**: *Si je travaillais bien, je réussirais.*   If I worked well, I **would succeed.**

Some verbs like *devoir* (to have to), *pouvoir* (to be able to), *savoir* (to know how to) and *vouloir* (to want) are often seen in the conditional in *si* clauses:

> *Si vous étiez riche, vous voudriez voyager.*   If you **were** rich, you **would like** to travel.

You can also use the conditional of *pouvoir* to suggest a future event:

> *On pourrait aller au ciné?*   We **could** go to the cinema?

Practise using *si* clauses and to try to incorporate them into your spoken and written French.

> ⭐ Don't try to use the perfect tense after *si*: it must be the imperfect tense.

H 1 Add the correct ending to each verb.

1 Si tu viens, j'ir_____ aussi.

2 Si vous arrivez à l'heure, nous sortir_____ ensemble.

3 Si j'avais beaucoup d'argent, j'achèter_____ des cadeaux.

4 Si elle était plus travailleuse, elle aur_____ de bonnes notes.

5 Si nous arrivons tôt, vous ser_____ content.

6 Si j'allais en Suisse, je fer_____ du ski.

> ⭐ Remember that if the first verb is in the present tense, you'll need the future tense ending for the second verb; but if the first verb is in the imperfect tense, you'll need the conditional ending for the second verb.

H 2 Put the verbs in brackets into the correct tense.

1 Si je vais en ville, je _____ (*manger*) avec toi.

2 Si elle _____ (*gagner*) la loterie, elle ira en vacances.

3 Si vous êtes en retard, nous _____ (*attendre*) devant la gare.

4 Si tu _____ (*venir*) au cinéma, nous pourrons voir le film ensemble.

5 Si on va au cinéma, on _____ (*regarder*) un film d'action.

6 Si elles _____ (*faire*) beaucoup d'effort, elles auront de bonnes notes.

> ⭐ All the clauses in this exercise use *si* + the present + the future.

H 3 Put the verbs in brackets into the correct tense.

1 Si tu sortais, j'_____ (*aller*) avec toi.

2 Si elle _____ (*faire*) les magasins, elle serait plus contente.

3 Si tu allais à l'université, tu _____ (*trouver*) un meilleur emploi.

4 Si elles _____ (*travailler*) dur, elles réussiraient.

5 Si je gagnais beaucoup d'argent, je _____ (*visiter*) plein de pays différents.

6 Si nous _____ (*aller*) en vacances, j'achèterais des souvenirs.

> ⭐ This time all the sentences use *si* + the imperfect + the conditional.

84

Studio GCSE French © Pearson Education Limited 2016

H 4 **Translate these sentences into English.**
They all include modal verbs in the conditional.

1 Si je révise beaucoup j'aurai de bonnes notes.

....

2 Si elle a de la chance, elle trouvera un bon emploi.

> *avoir de la chance* = to be lucky

....

3 Si vous mangiez moins de sucre, vous seriez en forme.

....

4 Si nous regardions moins de télé, nous pourrions lire plus de romans.

....

H 5 **Translate these sentences into French.**

1 If my friends arrive soon, we'll go to the shops.

> 'We'll' is 'we will' – future tense.

....

2 If I won the lottery, I'd like to visit Brazil.

> 'I'd' is 'I would' – conditional tense.

....

3 If he studied, he would be able to go to university.

....

H 6 **Translate this passage into French.**

> Use *on* here, with the *il/elle* ending of the verb.

If we found a job in a shop, we would have some money. I would like to go to a concert in France and you would be able to buy a car. If my friends have enough money, they will go to the concert too. It will be great.

> a form of *pouvoir*

> Watch out for the tenses in this sentence!

> How would you say 'also' in French?

....

....

....

....

....

G You need to use interrogatives (question words) to ask certain types of question. As you have seen, this is useful when you want to ask questions in a role play and it is also important to be able to recognise them when you need to answer questions.

question word	English meaning
qui?	who?
quand?	when?
où?	where?
comment?	how?
combien de?	how much / many?
à quelle heure?	at what time?
pourquoi?	why?
que?	what?
depuis quand?	since when / for how long?

There are three different ways of asking questions in French using interrogatives:

1. The interrogative can start the question and may be followed by *est-ce que*:

   Où est-ce que tu habites?   **Where** do you live?
   Qu'est-ce que tu veux faire?   **What** do you want to do?

2. If you prefer, you can turn the subject and verb around after the interrogative:

   Où habites-tu?   **Where** do you live?

3. Alternatively, you can just use voice intonation or add a question mark to the end of a statement to show that it is a question:

   Où tu habites? or *Tu habites où?*

Some ways are easier than others; you should use the ones you feel comfortable with, but be able to recognise them all.

1 Complete the sentences with the correct interrogative.

1 À Quelle heure ✓ _____ (*At what time*) vas-tu arriver?

2 _____ quand ✓ _____ (*When*) es-tu parti?

3 _____ où ✓ _____ (*Where*) est-ce que vous allez en vacances normalement?

4 _____ qui ✓ _____ (*Who*) aime le sport?

5 _____ combien de ✓ _____ (*How many*) de frères as-tu?

2 Match up the question halves.

1 Qu'
2 Comment
3 Pourquoi
4 À quelle heure
5 Où
6 Quand
7 Combien de
8 Depuis quand

a tu t'appelles? 2 ✓
b est-ce que tu te réveilles? 4 ✓
c allez-vous en vacances? 5 ✓
d personnes habitent à Londres? 7 ✓
e as-tu vu l'homme? 6 ✓
f apprends-tu le français? 8 ✓
g aimez-vous le rugby? 3 ✓
h est-ce que tu aimes faire? 1 ✓

Studio GCSE French © Pearson Education Limited 2016

3 Match up the French and the English questions.

1 Où travaille ton père? d ✓
2 Combien d'amis as-tu sur Facebook? a ✓
3 Pourquoi as-tu quitté la maison? f ✓
4 Que voulez-vous faire? c ✓
5 Comment s'appelle son copain? b ✓
6 Qui a fait cela? e ✓

a How many friends do you have on Facebook?
b What is your friend's name?
c What do you want to do?
d Where does your father work?
e Who did that?
f Why did you leave the house?

4 Translate these questions into English.

1 Quand es-tu allé en ville?

When did you go into town? ✓

2 Pourquoi est-ce qu'il aime le sport?

Why does he like sport? ✓

3 Depuis quand habites-tu en Angleterre?

How long have you lived in England for?

> You don't translate *est-ce que* word for word.

> Remember that the present tense used with *depuis* is translated as a past tense in English.

4 Où est-ce que tu travailleras?

where are you going to work? ✓

5 Combien de fois par semaine fais-tu du judo?

How many times a week do you do judo?

5 Translate these questions into French.

1 How do you get to school? Comment allez-vous à l'école? ✓

2 What did you do yesterday? Qu'est-ce que vous avez fait hier? ✓

3 At what time does she arrive at school?

À quelle heure arrive-t-elle à l'école ✓

> You don't use a word for 'does' in French.

6 Translate this passage into French.

> Use *on* here.

> This needs a singular verb.

What do you want to do? Where do people usually go on holiday? How many times a year does your family go to France? For how long have you been visiting Switzerland? When did they go skiing? Where will you go on holiday next year? What was your last holiday like?

> You will need to use the verb for 'visit' in the present tense.

> Use *comment* in this sentence and remember that holiday will be plural in French.

Que est-ce que voulez-vous faire? Où va-t-on en vacances? Combien de fois par an va-t-elle votre famille en France? Pour combien de temps visite-tu en Suisse? Quand allé-ils skier? Où va aller-tu pendant les vacances l'année prochaine?

(G) Prepositions are useful words for making your speaking and writing clear and accurate. They tell you where something is.

Here are some common prepositions:

à	to / at	*depuis*	since	*sous*	under
après	after	*derrière*	behind	*vers*	towards
avant	before	*devant*	in front of	*à côté de*	beside / next to
avec	with	*entre*	between	*près de*	near
chez	at the house of	*pendant*	during	*en face de*	opposite
contre	against	*pour*	for	*à cause de*	because of
dans	in	*sans*	without	*au lieu de*	instead of
de	from	*sur*	on		

⭐ *Chez* can be used to talk about places like shops and surgeries: e.g. ***chez** le médecin* (at the doctor's). It is also used for countries in statements such as ***Chez** nous, on parle français* (In my country, we speak French).

Note that *à* changes to *au*, *à la*, *à l'* or *aux*, depending on the noun which follows:

masculine:	*au cinéma*	to / at the cinema
feminine:	*à la gare*	to / at the station
word starting with a vowel or silent *h*:	*à l'hôpital*	to / at the hospital
plural:	*aux magasins*	to / at the shops

Similarly, *de* changes to *du*, *de la*, *de l'* or *des*, depending on the noun which follows:

masculine:	*à côté **du** collège*	next to the school
feminine:	*près **de la** piscine*	near the swimming pool
word starting with a vowel or silent *h*:	*en face **de** l'hôtel*	opposite the hotel
plural:	*en face **des** supermarchés*	opposite the supermarkets

1 **Complete the sentences with the correct prepositions. Choose from *à*, *au*, *à la*, *à l'* or *aux*.**

1 Je vais _____ Paris.

2 Elle va _____ musée.

3 Nous allons _____ église.

4 Ils vont _____ restaurants.

5 Tu vas _____ patinoire.

⭐ Look carefully at the last word in each sentence.

2 **Complete the sentences with the correct prepositions. Choose from *de*, *du*, *de la*, *de l'* or *des*.**

1 Je suis en face _____ bibliothèque.

2 Nous sommes à côté _____ hôtel de ville.

3 Elle part _____ Madrid.

4 Vous êtes près _____ commerces.

5 Ils sont en face _____ château.

3 **Write these sentences in the correct order.**

1 sommes devant la Nous gare.

_____

2 vais cinéma mes avec copains Je au.

_____

3 est musée derrière Elle le.

_____

4 près magasins suis Je des.

_____

5 passer jours vais mon chez copain Je deux.

_____

6 au après toi Elles collège arrivent.

_____

4 Translate these sentences into English.

1 La mosquée est entre le centre commercial et le bowling.

2 Il y a un jardin public en face de l'office de tourisme.

3 Notre maison est près du marché.

4 J'ai laissé mes cahiers sur la table.

5 Translate these sentences into French.

1 My flat is behind the bank.

2 There is a museum next to the town hall.

3 I went to the department store with my family.

'Department store' is masculine in French.

H 6 Translate this passage into French.

Decide if you need *qui* or *que*. Think: does it replace the subject or object?

You need the imperfect tense here.

Yesterday I went to the library which is next to the police station. I was walking towards the theatre when I noticed some friends opposite the petrol station. We went to my house, then we played football in the park in front of the factory.

If you don't know the French for 'noticed', what could you use here instead?

Not 'ma maison', so what should it be?

Conjunctions   Coordinating conjunctions

G You use conjunctions to join short sentences to increase their complexity. They are easy to use as they usually just involve remembering an item of vocabulary and using it.

These are all coordinating conjunctions and you are likely to use them frequently:

- *car*   because
  Je veux jouer au foot car c'est ma passion.   I want to play football **because** it's my passion.
- *donc*   so
  Tu es paresseux, donc tu ne fais rien.   You're lazy **so** you don't do anything.
- *ensuite*   next/then
  Je vais au ciné, ensuite je prends un verre dans un café.   I go to the cinema, **then** I have a drink in a café.
- *et*   and
  J'ai des livres et j'ai des cahiers.   I have text books **and** I have exercise books.
- *mais*   but
  Elle a une gomme mais elle n'a pas de stylo.   She has a rubber **but** she hasn't got a pen.
- *or*   now, yet
  Il était sûr de gagner, or il a perdu.   He was sure of winning, **yet** he lost.
- *ou*   or
  Il veut aller en vacances en Allemagne ou en France.   He wants to go on holiday to Germany **or** France.
- *ou bien*   or else
  Il étudiera le français ou bien il fera un apprentissage.   He will study French **or else** he will do an apprenticeship.
- *puis*   then
  On se lève puis on se lave.   We get up, **then** we get washed.
- *ne...ni...ni*   neither...nor
  Nous n'aimons ni l'anglais ni les maths.   We like **neither** English **nor** maths.

As in the example above (*ni...ni*), you can use coordinating conjunctions for emphasis by repeating them:

- *et...et*   both...and
  Je connais et ton père et ta mère.   I know **both** your mother **and** your father.
- *ou...ou*   either...or
  Elles vont ou regarder un film ou écouter de la musique.   They're going to **either** watch a film **or** listen to some music.

1 Match up the French and English conjunctions.

1	ou....ou	a	then
2	et...et	b	neither...nor
3	ne...ni...ni	c	so
4	donc	d	either...or
5	puis	e	both...and

2 Complete the sentences with a conjunction from the box.

1 J'aime lire, _____ j'achète beaucoup de romans.

2 Je n'aime ni les sciences _____ les maths.

3 Je prends le petit-déjeuner, _____ je m'habille.

4 J'adore les pommes _____ je déteste les poires.

5 Il veut aller en France _____ en Espagne.

6 Nous aimons le français _____ c'est utile.

mais
ni
donc
car
ou
puis

⭐ Make sure the sentence makes sense when you've filled the gap!

Studio GCSE French © Pearson Education Limited 2016

3 **Complete the sentences with an appropriate conjunction.**

1 Elle est fatiguée, _____ elle se repose.

2 Nous mangeons beaucoup de fruits _____
   ils sont pleins de vitamines.

3 Il boit du coca _____ de la limonade.

4 Ils vont aller en ville _____ jouer au foot.

5 J'aime le rugby _____ je déteste le tennis.

6 Je me lève _____ je me lave.

4 **Translate these sentences into English.**

1 Je vais souvent en ville car j'aime faire les magasins.

_____

2 Elles n'aiment ni la lecture ni l'équitation.

_____

3 J'adore jouer au hockey mais je déteste faire du VTT.

_____

4 Nous dînons, ensuite nous regardons la télé, puis nous faisons nos devoirs.

_____

5 **Translate these sentences into French.**

1 I know both his uncle and his aunt.

_____

2 He has two brothers but no sisters.

_____

3 My friends play badminton or volleyball.

_____

> Which conjunction will you need to use here?

> You can translate 'no' by making *il a* negative, but don't forget that *de* follows a negative.

H **6** **Translate this passage into French.**

> You don't translate 'On' here.

> Use *faire* in the perfect tense here.

On Saturdays I either go to the ice rink or watch a film at the cinema. Last weekend I went shopping because I wanted some new clothes. I saw a green dress, so I bought it. Next week I'm going to play on my computer but I'm not going to study!

> This is *de* here.

> As 'dress' is feminine in French, you will need to think about how to spell the past participle here, as it will need to agree.

_____

_____

_____

_____

_____

Conjunctions Subordinating conjunctions

G Subordinating conjunctions are words such as 'when', 'because', 'like', etc., which are used to join dependent clauses to main clauses. A **dependent clause** is a clause (including a conjunction) that cannot exist on its own:

<u>Je n'aime pas la physique</u> **parce que c'est nul**.   <u>I don't like physics</u> **because it's boring**.

The **dependent clause** is meaningless without the <u>main clause</u>.

Using these conjunctions can help to add complexity and variety to your written and spoken French.

Examples of subordinating conjunctions in French include:

- **comme**   as, like
  Comme *il est là, nous partirons.*   **As** he is here, we will leave.

- **lorsque**   when
  Lorsqu'*il neige, je suis content.*   **When** it snows, I'm happy.

- **parce que**   because
  Je voudrais être pilote **parce que** *c'est un emploi intéressant.*   I'd like to be a pilot **because** it's an interesting job.

- **puisque**   seeing that, since, as
  Puisqu'*elle aime voyager, elle va souvent à l'étranger.*   **Since** she likes travelling, she often goes abroad.

- **quand**   when
  Je vais au collège en car **quand** *il fait mauvais.*   I go to school by coach **when** the weather's bad.

- **que**   that
  Elle m'a dit **qu**'*elle préfère le dessin.*   She told me **that** she prefers art.

- **si**   if
  Si *je vais en ville, je ferai des achats.*   **If** I go into town I'll do some shopping.

H Remember that after *si* you need to use a sequence of tenses.

si + **the present** + <u>the future</u>:

S'il **fait** *chaud nous* <u>irons</u> *à la plage.*   If it **is** hot we <u>will go</u> to the beach.

si + **the imperfect** + <u>the conditional</u>:

Si je **gagnais** *le match, je* <u>serais</u> *content.*   If I **won** the match I <u>would be</u> pleased.

H *Quand* and *lorsque* are often followed by a **future tense** + <u>another future tense</u> when you are talking about the future. This is not the case in English, so it is important to remember this.

Lorsque je **serai** *en Espagne, je* <u>goûterai</u> *la cuisine régionale.*
When I **am** in Spain, I <u>will try</u> the local food.

1 Match up the French and English phrases.

1 quand je serai plus âgé
2 parce qu'il y fait chaud
3 comme j'aime jouer au golf
4 puisque je n'aime pas manger de fruits
5 si je pouvais finir mes devoirs

a as I like playing golf
b when I'm older
c since I don't like eating fruit
d if I could finish my homework
e because it's hot there

2 Fill in the gaps with an appropriate conjunction from the box.

1 Elle adore les randonnées _____ elle est très active.

2 _____ je suis paresseux, j'aime être devant la télé.

3 Elle a dit _____ c'était intéressant.

4 _____ il pleut, je mets mon imperméable.

5 _____ je suis un peu gros, je dois éviter le sucre.

H 6 _____ je travaille dur, j'aurai de bonnes notes.

comme
quand
si
puisque
que
parce que

Studio GCSE French © Pearson Education Limited 2016

H 3 Match up the sentence halves.

1 Quand on part en famille
2 J'aime aller en France
3 Nous évitons le fast-food
4 Si on mange plus équilibré
5 Je pense

a puisque c'est mauvais pour la santé.
b on sera en meilleure forme.
c on va au bord de la mer.
d que c'est barbant.
e parce que j'adore parler français.

4 Translate these sentences into English.

1 Tu aimes les sciences parce que c'est une matière utile.

_____

2 Quand elle quittera la fac, elle sera professeur de biologie.

_____

3 Nous savons qu'elle voudrait être architecte.

_____

4 Si tu joues bien, tu gagneras le match.

_____

5 Translate these sentences into French.

1 He thinks that rugby is violent.

_____

2 Since he likes cars, he is a mechanic.

> No word for 'a' with jobs.

_____

3 We hate art because it's boring.

_____

H 6 Translate this passage into French.

> 'To pass' is *réussir*, not *passer*.

> This will be a future tense in French.

> Use the correct form of *avoir l'intention de* + infinitive.

If I pass my exams I'd like to work in France because it's a beautiful country. When I am older I intend to become an engineer since I think that science is important. As I'm good at maths, it was my favourite subject at school.

> Think carefully about the adjective here!

> Which past tense do you need here?

_____

_____

_____

_____

You will use the present and perfect tenses a great deal in French so the more you practise them, the better. You will also need to be able to recognise them in reading and listening exercises, so it is useful to look out for clues to distinguish between them.

The present tense

The present tense usually has just one part of the verb (*je vais*, *elle mange*, *nous parlons*). However, you will need to remember that it can be translated into English in a number of different ways: *je vais* could be 'I go', 'I am going' or 'I do go', depending on the context.

Remember, there is no word for 'is/am/are' in French when you translate the continuous present – 'he is going/I am going/we are going', etc. If you need a reminder of how to form the present tense, have a look at p. 40 and p. 42.

I **am going** to play football.   *Je **vais** jouer au foot.*

The perfect tense

The perfect tense is used for completed, single actions in the past: 'I went', 'you saw', 'they ran', etc. For a reminder of how to use the perfect tense, see p. 50 and p. 52.

Remember that the perfect tense has two parts: a part of *avoir* or *être* and the past participle:

*j'ai **fait***   I have done   *elle a **regardé***   she watched   *nous avons **vu***   we saw

If the verb takes *être*, the past participle must agree: e.g. ***elle*** *est **allée*** (see p. 52 to remind yourself).

Looking for clues

In reading and listening texts you might need to identify if a verb is in the past or not. As well as knowing how each tense is formed, contextual clues can help. Time phrases such as *la semaine dernière* (last week), *le week-end dernier* (last weekend), *hier* (yesterday) and *il y a deux jours* (two days ago) will indicate a past tense, whereas you might see words like *maintenant* or *généralement* for a present tense.

1 Identify the tense of the verbs in these sentences. Present or perfect?

> ★ Be careful – the perfect uses the present tense of *avoir* or *être*, but make sure to look for a past participle too!

1   Je suis anglais. _____

2   Hier je suis allé en Espagne. _____

3   J'aime manger du poisson. _____

4   Hier soir ils ont mangé trop tard. _____

5   Le week-end dernier nous avons vu un film au cinéma. _____

6   Elle va au collège à pied. _____

2 Complete the sentences with the correct form of either the present or perfect tense of the verb in brackets.

> ★ Remember in the perfect tense, if a verb takes *être* you must make the past participle agree with the subject of the sentence. See p. 50 and p. 52 to remind yourself which verbs take *avoir* and which take *être* in the perfect tense.

1   Elle _____ (*lire* – present) beaucoup.

2   Tu _____ (*aimer* – present) le sport?

3   Nous _____ (*manger* – perfect) un repas délicieux.

4   Il _____ (*jouer* – present) du piano.

5   Ils _____ (*acheter* – perfect) des cadeaux.

6   Mohammed _____ (*écouter* – perfect) la radio.

7   Elles _____ (*aller* – perfect) en ville.

8   Vous _____ (*sortir* – perfect) à huit heures.

> ★ Remember DR + MRS VAN DER TRAMP verbs use *être* as auxiliary verb in the perfect tense and the past participle must agree with the subject. Try to learn these 16 verbs by heart if you can.

3 Rewrite the sentences in the correct order and then translate them into English.

1 en Suisse suis allé Je. ....

....

2 sommes dans salon Nous entrés le. ....

....

3 aime au jouer tennis Elle. ....

....

4 parles avec copains Tu tes. ....

....

5 Ils de heure bonne partis sont. ....

....

> ⭐ Be careful: three words in French can be translated by one in English.

> ⭐ It is important to get the translation right when there are two tenses in one sentence. Look out for time indicators for the present and past: e.g. *maintenant* → now.

4 Translate these sentences into English.

1 Normalement je vais en vacances en France mais l'année dernière je suis allé en Italie.

....

2 J'ai étudié le dessin mais maintenant je préfère les maths.

....

3 Aujourd'hui je joue au basket mais hier j'ai joué au volley.

....

4 D'habitude je vais au collège à pied, mais ce matin j'ai pris l'autobus.

....

> ⭐ Each sentence has a verb in the present tense and one in the perfect.

5 Translate these sentences into French.

1 Last weekend I played badminton but I prefer rugby.

....

2 I have a laptop but yesterday I bought a tablet.

....

3 I like documentaries but last week I watched a game show.

....

> Think carefully about how to translate 'played'.

> Use this as a clue to the tense which follows.

🅗 6 Translate this passage into French.

> Use the correct form of *faire*.

Today my brother is tired because he went rock-climbing yesterday. Last week I went roller skating but I prefer horse-riding. My friends hate sport but like music. Last weekend we went to a concert. Do you like sport?

> Remember that this will need a plural verb.

> Remember, you can just translate 'you like sport' and add a question mark to make a question.

....

....

....

G It is really important to be able to demonstrate that you can use a variety of tenses in your written and spoken French, particularly as this can show complexity and accuracy. As your teacher will often tell you, an ability to use tenses from a number of time frames (past, present and future) can be impressive.

- Use the perfect tense to say what somebody <u>did</u> or <u>has done</u> in the past:
  *Il **a travaillé** très dur.*   He **worked** very hard.

- Use the present tense to talk about <u>now</u> and say what you <u>usually</u> do:
  *Je **vais** à la bibliothèque tous les jours.*   **I go** to the library every day.

- Use the near future to say what you're <u>going to do</u>:
  *Je **vais regarder** un film.*   **I am going** to watch a film.

Looking and listening for time phrases as well as tenses can help you to identify whether somebody is referring to the past, present or future. You should use them in your spoken and written work to provide suitable contexts for what you produce. Here are some common time phrases:

past	present	future
hier yesterday	*d'habitude* usually	*demain* tomorrow
le week-end dernier last weekend	*normalement* normally	*le week-end prochain* next weekend
la semaine dernière last week	*en général* in general, generally, usually	*la semaine prochaine* next week
l'année dernière last year	*maintenant* now	*l'année prochaine* next year

Note that *aujourd'hui* (today) could be used with all three tenses.

It is sometimes obvious that three tenses are needed:

Hier *il a fait chaud,* **aujourd'hui** *il pleut,* **demain** *il va y avoir du soleil.*
Yesterday it was hot, **today** it's raining and **tomorrow** it's going to be sunny.

1 Identify the tense of the verbs in these sentences: perfect, present or near future?

1 Le week-end dernier je suis allé au bord de la mer. _____

2 Demain nous allons faire du judo. _____

3 Je mange mon sandwich chez moi. _____

4 Hier il s'est levé vers midi. _____

5 J'ai quinze ans. _____

6 Plus tard nous allons jouer au foot. _____

2 Find the verbs in the passage and highlight them using a different colour for each tense.

J'habite dans une grande ville industrielle. Il y a beaucoup de déchets dans les rues. Mes amis et moi avons décidé de faire quelque chose pour aider l'environnement, alors nous avons ramassé les papiers et les bouteilles vides au centre-ville et les avons mis dans des poubelles. La semaine prochaine mon meilleur ami, Paul, va écrire au maire et nous allons l'inviter à venir voir ce que nous avons fait.

3 Complete this passage by putting the infinitives in brackets into the correct tense.

⭐ Look for clues in each of the sentences. Pay attention to time phrases and think carefully about the meaning.

Normalement tous les samedis je **1** _____ (*faire*)

du karaté, mais samedi dernier je **2** _____ (*aller*)

à Rouen avec ma famille. Nous y **3** _____ (*visiter*) un musée célèbre. Le week-end prochain je

4 _____ (*participer*) à un concours de judo.

4 Translate these sentences into English.

⭐ It is important to be able to translate from French into English with precision, especially when more than one tense is being used.

1 Ce matin j'ai nagé, cet après-midi je fais du cyclisme et ce soir je vais aller à la pêche.

2 Hier il a loué un vélo et demain il va visiter tous les monuments historiques.

3 D'habitude je lis un magazine avant de me coucher mais ce soir je vais écouter la radio.

4 Le week-end dernier elles sont allées à un concert et dimanche prochain elles vont voir un spectacle.

Théâtre de la Ville
Chausson, Debussy, Fauré
5 décembre · F22
F23

⭐ Take care when forming all your tenses. Look back over the grammar pages for the perfect (see p. 50 and p. 52), present (p. 40 and p. 42) and near future (see p. 60) if you need to remind yourself.

5 Translate these sentences into French.

1 Yesterday I went skiing and today I'm going to go windsurfing.

Use *faire* for both verbs here.

2 On Mondays she plays table tennis but next weekend she's going to play tennis.

3 Last year we went to Italy but next year we are going to visit New York.

en or *à*?

ℍ 6 Translate this passage into French.

trop de

There is too much traffic in my town. It's very dangerous. Yesterday my dad wrote a letter to the newspaper. Next week we are going to start an online petition to reduce the number of cars and lorries on the roads.

This will come after 'petition' in French.

You will need another word before the infinitive.

le nombre de

You will need a preposition here as well.

G
H Just as it is impressive to use the **present**, **perfect** and **near future** tenses together, it is even better if you can successfully use four tenses, with the addition of the **imperfect** tense.

- The **present tense** is used when talking about things that are <u>happening now</u> or things that <u>usually happen</u>.
- The **perfect tense** is used for <u>completed, simple actions in the past</u>: 'I went', 'you saw', 'they ran', etc.
- Use the **near future** to talk about what you are <u>going to do</u> or events which are <u>going to happen soon</u>.
- The **imperfect tense** is used to describe what <u>was happening</u>, what <u>used to happen</u> or what was <u>ongoing</u> when something happened.

You might want to discuss past, present and future events and compare what you used to do in the past with what you do now, thus adding the imperfect tense to the mixture. If you can do this correctly and accurately, it demonstrates an even greater awareness of structure.

If you need to remind yourself of the differences between how you form and use each of the tenses, look back at pp. 40–47 for the present tense, pp. 50–55 for the perfect tense, pp. 56–57 for the imperfect tense and pp. 60–61 for the near future tense. Alternatively, refer to the verb tables on pp. 124–128.

1 **Match up the French and the English phrases.**

1 Il y a une patinoire en ville.

2 Il y avait une gare dans mon village.

3 On va aller au stade.

4 Nous sommes allés à l'église.

a We went to church.

b There is an ice rink in town.

c There used to be a station in my village.

d We are going to go to the stadium.

2 **Complete the sentences with the correct form and tense of the verb in brackets.**

1 Tu _____ (*mettre – perfect*) tes chaussures noires.

2 Elle _____ (*avoir – present*) de la chance.

3 Vous _____ (*finir – present*) les devoirs.

4 Tu _____ (*aller jouer – near future*) au basket.

5 Ils _____ (*faire – perfect*) du ski.

6 Nous _____ (*boire – present*) beaucoup d'eau minérale.

7 Je _____ (*être – imperfect*) content.

H 8 Je _____ (*manger – imperfect*) à la cantine.

H **3** **Complete the sentences with the correct word from the box.**

1 Mon copain _____ bientôt arriver chez moi.

2 Hier nous _____ à la campagne.

3 Je _____ toujours avant sept heures.

4 Il y a deux ans ils _____ de la gymnastique le dimanche.

5 Vous _____ au café ce matin.

6 En été on _____ la France avec la famille.

> visitait
>
> sommes allés
>
> va
>
> faisaient
>
> avez mangé
>
> me lève

4 Translate these sentences into English.

1 Quand j'étais jeune je jouais au babyfoot.

2 Je n'aimais pas les légumes mais je les adore maintenant.

3 Le 14 juillet nous regardions les feux d'artifice mais maintenant nous habitons en Angleterre.

4 Elle a préparé un gâteau au chocolat et ce soir je vais en manger.

H 5 Translate these sentences into French.

1 We used to have a flat but last year we bought a house.

2 He was doing his homework when the postman came.

3 I am going to go on a school exchange in spring and I am very happy.

Remember, there is no word for 'used to' or 'was' in French; you just need the correct tense of the verb.

H 6 Translate this passage into French.

This will be singular in French – take care with the verb that follows it.

There is a variety of tenses in this passage, so look carefully at the verbs and use any time phrases to help you decide which tense to use.

In September I'm going to leave school. We have worked well and everyone has had good marks. When I was younger I used to like every subject but next year I am going to study physics and my friend, Janine, is going to find a job. My best friend was going to study at university but now he has a job in a bank.

Here are some useful strategies to help you translate from French into English. As you are doing the translations on the following pages, refer back to these strategies to help you.

Reading for gist

When you are faced with a passage or sentence to translate from French into English, it is really important to read through each sentence in order to establish the general meaning, even if you know that there are some words you don't recognise or cannot immediately translate.

Breaking it down

- Next, look at each sentence or phrase. Try to group words or phrases that logically go together, and produce an English translation that sounds right.

  Facebook est ➜ *le réseau social* ➜ *le plus populaire* ➜ *au monde.*
  Facebook is the most popular social network in the world.

  Remember that word order can be different in French and English – you wouldn't say 'Facebook is the social network most popular in the world'.

- You will need to remember that adjectives usually come <u>after</u> the word they describe in French. So, if you had to translate *Elle porte une écharpe rose,* you would write 'She is wearing a <u>pink scarf</u>', not 'a scarf pink'.

- Watch out for object pronouns when translating, as the word order is different in French to what you would expect in English. Be especially careful of *le, la, l'* or *les* meaning 'him', 'her', 'it' or 'them', as they will come <u>before</u> the verb and must not be confused with the French words for 'the', which are identical.

  *Je **le** donne à Marc.*   I give **it** to Marc. | Don't be tempted to translate *le* as 'the' here. |

Using familiar language, context and common sense

- Try to use familiar language, context and common sense to decode the meaning of words you don't know. In the following sentence, identify the words you <u>definitely</u> know:

  Elle déteste partager sa chambre avec sa sœur.

  You probably recognise *elle déteste* (she hates), *sa chambre* (her bedroom) and *avec sa sœur* (with her sister). You might also know *partager*, but if you don't, use the vocabulary you do know to make an informed guess. So far you have 'She hates … her bedroom with her sister'. Ask yourself: what makes sense in the context of the rest of the text? Given that there is just one word in French, the English translation will probably only be one or two words, so you wouldn't guess something long like 'going on the computer' and it can't be something which you already know the French for, such as 'watching TV' or 'reading'. You might guess the correct answer – 'sharing' or 'to share'.

  Now look at this sentence:

  Je vais à la pêche avec mes copains.

  You might know that *pêche* has two meanings in French ('fishing' and 'peach'), but in this context, common sense tells you that only one would work: 'I go fishing with my friends'.

Using cognates and near cognates

- Look for <u>cognates</u> (words which are the same in both languages (e.g. 'confusion', 'suggestion', 'biscuit') or <u>near cognates</u> (words which are very similar in both languages (e.g. *ridicule* (ridiculous), *commencer* (to commence), *difficile* (difficult)), as you can easily work out the meaning of these words in English, even if you might not have known the word if you had been asked to translate it from English into French.

- You can sometimes work out the meaning of a word which is a near-cognate and then adapt it to get a better translation.

  *Elle sert les **clients** au café.*

  'Clients' is also an English word, but a more natural translation here would be 'she serves the <u>customers</u> at the café'.

False Friends

- Watch out for 'false friends': French words which look similar to English, but actually have totally different meanings. Look at these sentences:

  *Mon frère est très **sensible**.*   *Elle **travaille** à l'étranger.*   *La **journée** était fatigante.*

  If you think about cognates or near-cognates, you might have tried the following translations:

  My brother is very **sensible**. She **travels** abroad. The **journey** was tiring.

  All three would be wrong! The correct translations are:

  My brother is very **sensitive**. She **works** abroad. The day was **tiring**.

Grammar

- Use **tense indicators** and your <u>grammatical knowledge</u> to help you translate into the correct tense:

Present: ***D'habitude**, <u>je vais</u> au collège à pied.*   **Usually** <u>I walk</u> to school.
Past: ***Le week-end dernier**, <u>nous sommes allés</u> en ville.*   **Last weekend** <u>we went</u> to town.
Future: ***Demain**, <u>nous allons aller</u> au théâtre.*   **Tomorrow** <u>we are going to go</u> to the theatre.

- Remember that you can translate some tenses in more than one way. Try out the various versions and see which sounds better in the context:

Present: *Je prends mon petit déjeuner* ➔   I eat breakfast <u>or</u> I am eating breakfast

Perfect: *J'ai pris mon petit déjeuner* ➔   I ate breakfast <u>or</u> I have eaten breakfast

Imperfect: *Je prenais mon petit déjeuner* ➔   I ate breakfast <u>or</u> I was eating breakfast <u>or</u> I used to eat breakfast

Translation skills

- Don't always try to translate word for word. This can cause real problems, as you won't always find that one word in French means one word in English.

  Il y a deux salles de bains chez moi.   There are two bathrooms in my house.

  Il y a ➔ there is/are   *deux salles de bains* ➔ two bathrooms   *chez moi* ➔ in my house

  Also, don't forget that singular nouns in French might equate to plural nouns in English, or vice versa:

  *Ce soir, je vais faire **mes devoirs**.*   This evening I am going to do **my homework**.

- Sometimes you might have to <u>paraphrase</u> (find a phrase that has the same meaning, but uses different words) to complete a translation that sounds natural in English.

  Pour elle, le bonheur c'est la danse.

  Here, a great translation in English would be 'Dancing is what makes her happy'. A word for word translation would sound very strange in English: 'For her, the joy is the dance!'.

- Don't be afraid to use <u>different words</u> or a <u>different number</u> of words to get a good translation. However, don't stray too far from the meaning or make random guesses.

  It is, however, important <u>to account</u> for every word in a translation, even if some words don't need translating or if you need to add words for the sentence to make sense.

  Look at these examples:

  *Ils jouent **au** foot le weekend.*

  They play football **at** the weekend.

  > You don't need to translate *'au'* into English but 'at' has been added for the sentence to make sense.

  *Je vais regarder **la** télé demain soir.*

  I'm going to watch TV tomorrow evening.

  > *la* (the) is not needed in English.

- Make sure that you read your translation to yourself (out loud if you can) to check that it makes sense and sounds natural. For example, you could translate *J'aime aussi jouer au tennis* as 'I also like playing tennis' or 'I like playing tennis too', but not as 'I like also playing tennis', as this sounds clumsy in English.
  Play around with the word order until your English translation sounds natural.

1a Read the passage about Thomas's hobbies. Translate the words below into English.

> Moi, j'adore faire du vélo, surtout le week-end avec mes copains. J'aime aussi regarder la télé et je préfère les dessins animés car ils sont amusants. Je déteste faire des achats et je n'aime pas faire des promenades parce que c'est très ennuyeux.

1 surtout _es_ _____

2 aussi _al_ _____

3 les dessins animés _____

4 car _____

5 faire des achats _____

6 ennuyeux _____

b Now translate the whole text into English.

_____

_____

_____

_____

> Try reading the passage to yourself before attempting to translate it. Identify any words you don't already know. Can you work them out from the context?

2a Read this text about Amélie's family.

> Je m'appelle Amélie et je vais vous parler de ma famille. J'ai un petit frère qui s'appelle Luc et il m'énerve. Je m'entends bien avec ma sœur, Caroline, qui a douze ans. Elle est jolie et généreuse. Ma mère est gentille et nous allons souvent au centre sportif ensemble.

b Someone has translated the passage but has made mistakes. Correct them if you can!

My name is Amélie and I **1 go** _am going_ to talk to you about my family. I have a little brother who is called Luc and he **2 is nervous** _annoys me_ . I get on well with my sister, Caroline, who is **3 10** _12_ years old. She is **4 jolly** _pretty_ and generous. My mum is kind and we **5 go often** _often go_ to the sports centre together.

3 Now translate the following two passages into English.

1 En juillet chaque année, il y a un festival de musique dans ma ville. Tout a commencé il y a dix ans mais maintenant, le festival est plus grand et plus important. Pourtant, à mon avis, il y a trop de touristes.

In July the y _____ _music festival_

_____

_____

_____

2 Ma meilleure copine, Jennifer, passe beaucoup de temps à faire de l'équitation. Elle a un cheval gris mais elle en voudrait un autre. Je me passionne pour les sports d'hiver et je vais aller en Italie faire du ski en janvier.

> When you have completed your translation, read it out loud to make sure that it sounds natural. If it doesn't, then make some changes.

_____

_____

4 As a practice for translating passages from French to English, here is a passage which has been partly translated. Fill in the gaps with the correct English translation.

> Ma passion, c'est faire du VTT. J'en fais presque tous les jours et selon moi c'est non seulement bon pour la forme mais aussi intéressant parce qu'on peut apprécier le paysage et respirer l'air frais. Le week-end dernier, j'ai fait du vélo tout seul dans les belles collines près de chez moi.

(Can you think of a natural way of translating this?)   (How are you going to translate this?)

My passion is going **1** _mountain biking_ . I do this **2** _almost every day_
and in my opinion it's **3** _not only good exercise but it_
but also interesting because **4** _it helps you appreciate the views_
and fresh air . Last weekend I went cycling
5 _on beautiful hills near my house_ .

5 Translate these passages into English.

> Don't try to translate word for word. There might be times when you cannot do this. Remember too that word order can be different in French, as adjectives usually come <u>after</u> the word they describe.

1 Je sais que je ne pourrais pas vivre sans Internet. J'aime poster mes photos sur Facebook et rester en contact avec mes copains qui habitent loin de chez moi, même à l'étranger. Cependant, j'accepte qu'il y a des risques: par exemple, ma cousine a été victime de cyber-harcèlement et elle était vraiment inquiète.

2 J'ai plein d'amis, mais Mani est le meilleur. On a les mêmes centres d'intérêts, on bavarde, on va au ciné et bien qu'on se dispute de temps en temps, ce n'est jamais grave. Il est rigolo et compréhensif, alors on s'entend bien. Récemment, on est allés en vacances avec sa famille et tout le monde s'est bien amusé.

3 J'habite dans le sud-est de la France dans un petit village à la campagne. Le 14 juillet est la journée la plus importante de l'année pour nous. En général, il y a des compétitions sportives ou culturelles et le soir, on peut regarder un feu d'artifice, mais l'année prochaine, il y aura un cirque avec des animaux sauvages.

Translation: French–English

1a **Read the passage about Éric's local area.**

> J'habite dans une petite ville à la campagne. J'aime habiter ici parce que c'est tranquille et parce que beaucoup de mes amis habitent près de chez moi. On peut aller au cinéma et faire les magasins au centre-ville. Pourtant, je voudrais habiter en Espagne.

Can you try to think of a natural way to translate this phrase?

On would probably be best translated as 'you' here.

b **Find all the verbs in the passage and translate them into English.**

Try reading the passage to yourself before you attempt to translate it. Can you work out any words you don't know from the context?

....

....

....

C **Now translate the whole passage into English.**

....

....

....

2 **Read this text and complete the partial translation below.**

> Je m'appelle Jasmine et je vais vous parler de mes vacances. Normalement je vais en Suisse avec mes parents et nous passons une semaine dans les Alpes. Je fais du ski tous les jours mais ma sœur, qui a neuf ans, préfère rester à notre hôtel car elle n'est pas sportive.

My name is Jasmine and **1** .... about my holidays. Normally

2 .... with my parents and we **3** ....

in the Alps. I **4** .... but my sister, who **5** ....,

prefers to stay in our hotel because **6** ....

3 **Translate these two passages into English.**

When you have done your translation, read it aloud to make sure that it sounds natural. If it doesn't, then make some changes.

1 D'habitude je passe mes vacances dans un camping au pays de Galles avec ma famille. Nous voyageons en voiture et c'est mon père qui conduit. L'année dernière pendant le voyage j'ai écouté de la musique, mais mon petit frère a dormi.

....

....

2 J'habite dans un joli village au bord de la mer en Belgique. Je n'aime pas vivre ici car c'est barbant et il n'y a rien à faire pour les jeunes, mais de temps en temps je vais à la plage avec mes copains. Je préférerais habiter en France.

....

....

4 Look at this passage which has been translated into English. Would you have translated it in the same way? Remember that there is not just one correct translation.

> Ma ville est vraiment nulle. À mon avis c'est moche et tout le monde semble très triste. Il y a plein de choses à faire, mais les bâtiments sont vieux et tout est démodé. J'aimerais habiter dans une ville moderne, peut-être à l'étranger car je voudrais goûter à une culture différente.

Can you improve this translation?

How else could you translate *semble*?

Can you think of alternative translations for *plein de*?

> My town is really rubbish. In my opinion it's ugly and everyone seems very sad. There's a lot to do but the buildings are old and everything is old-fashioned. I'd like to live in a modern town, maybe abroad because I'd like to taste a different culture.

5 Translate these passages into English.

> ⭐ Don't try to translate word for word. There might be times when you can't do this. Remember too that word order can be different in French, as adjectives usually come <u>after</u> the word they describe.

1 L'année dernière je suis allé en vacances au Portugal avec mes parents, mais ma sœur aînée n'est pas venue car elle travaillait. Je me suis très bien amusé quand même parce qu'il y avait beaucoup à faire. Mes parents ont visité des musées et des monuments mais moi, j'ai bronzé et j'ai acheté des cadeaux.

2 J'aime voyager en avion car c'est un moyen de transport efficace, rapide et agréable. Ma tante a peur de prendre l'avion et il y a deux ans elle a refusé de nous accompagner en vacances. Par contre, je n'aime pas voyager en bateau parce que j'ai toujours le mal de mer.

3 Ma ville attire beaucoup de touristes à cause de son histoire. On peut visiter le château et la belle cathédrale mais pour ceux qui aiment le sport, il y a un stade de rugby où on peut regarder des matchs. J'y suis allé hier avec un copain anglais et c'était génial.

Translation: French–English Social issues and global issues

1 Read this passage about the *Tour de France* and correct the translation below.
The mistakes have been crossed out.

> Le *Tour de France* est l'événement sportif le plus important de France mais c'est aussi une compétition cycliste internationale. La course a lieu chaque année et des cyclistes de plus de cinquante nationalités différentes y ont participé depuis le commencement du Tour en 1903.

> The *Tour de France* is **1** ~~an important~~ .... sporting event in France but it's also
> **2** ~~a national~~ .... cycling competition. **3** ~~The course~~ .... takes
> place every year and cyclists from **4** ~~50 different nationalities~~ ....
> have taken part in it **5** ~~from~~ .... the start of the Tour in 1903.

2a Read what Louise says about recycling and translate the words below into English.

> J'essaie de tout recycler: le verre, le papier, le carton et le métal. Mes amis pensent qu'il est important de protéger notre planète et ils participent à des forums sur Internet. Récemment ma mère et moi avons commencé à recycler nos vieux vêtements.

1 recycler *to recycle*

2 le verre *bottle*

3 le carton *cartons*

4 protéger *protect*

5 notre planète *our planet*

6 nos vieux vêtements *Our old clothes*

b Now translate the whole passage into English.

I try to recycle all : bottles, paper, cartons and metal. My friends think that it is important to protect our planet and they participate in forums on the internet. Recently my mum and I started to recycle our old clothes.

3 Translate these passages into English.

1 Moi, je mange assez sainement et je ne bois pas de boissons gazeuses. L'année dernière, j'ai commencé à faire plus de sport et maintenant je suis en bonne forme physique. À l'avenir, je vais me coucher plus tôt en semaine.

2 Je pense qu'il faut réduire la pollution et économiser de l'énergie pour aider l'environnement. Je suis triste quand je vois les bons efforts des jeunes qui recyclent et utilisent les transports en commun alors que les gouvernements internationaux n'agissent pas assez.

Studio GCSE French © Pearson Education Limited 2016

4 **Read this passage about access to natural resources in Africa and correct the translation below. The mistakes have been crossed out.**

> Les ressources naturelles en Afrique de l'Ouest sont très importantes pour l'économie des pays francophones. Il y a beaucoup de forêts et de lacs, et le bois et le poisson apportent de l'argent des autres pays de la région et aussi des pays européens comme la France et la Belgique.

Natural resources in **1** ~~South~~ .... Africa are **2** ~~quite~~ .... important for the economies of French-speaking countries. There are **3** ~~some~~ .... forests and lakes, and **4** ~~cardboard~~ .... and fish bring in money from **5** ~~every country~~ .... in the area and also from European countries like France and Belgium.

5 **Translate these passages into English.**

1 Je m'intéresse beaucoup aux animaux et je suis membre d'une association caritative qui protège les animaux en danger de disparition dans le monde entier. Je travaille comme volontaire dans une ferme depuis plus de deux ans et je vais bientôt adopter un panda ou peut-être un tigre afin de conserver ces espèces.

2 Selon moi, fumer, boire de l'alcool et se droguer sont très mauvais pour la santé. Ma meilleure amie était accro à l'alcool mais j'ai essayé de la persuader de demander de l'aide. À l'avenir, elle essayera de ne plus boire d'alcool régulièrement et elle voudrait aider les autres à réduire leur consommation d'alcool.

3 Le changement climatique est pour moi le problème le plus grave au monde. Je m'inquiète des risques causés par le réchauffement de la Terre, surtout le niveau de la mer. Il y a eu plus d'inondations et de tempêtes partout et à mon avis, il faut qu'on réduise la pollution de l'atmosphère qui cause ces problèmes.

1 Read this passage and correct the translation below. The mistakes have been crossed out.

> Chaque année on peut faire un échange scolaire. Nous passons une semaine dans une ville dans le sud-est de l'Angleterre. L'année dernière j'ai participé à l'échange et c'était vraiment formidable. On a visité Londres où j'ai vu quelques monuments historiques et mon correspondant était sympa.

Every year you can go on a school exchange. We **1** ~~pass~~ _____ a week in a town in the **2** ~~south west~~ _____ of England. Last year I went on the exchange and it was **3** ~~quite good~~ _____. We visited London where I saw **4** ~~all the~~ _____ historic monuments and my partner was **5** ~~sympathetic~~ _____ .

2 Read this passage about a French school and correct the inaccurate translation below. The first sentence has been corrected for you as an example.

> Try to work out what *environ* means from the context.

> Mon collège est très grand et mixte. Il y a environ mille élèves âgés de onze à dix-huit ans. Mes professeurs sont assez stricts mais compréhensifs. J'ai trop de devoirs à faire tous les soirs.

> My college is very grand and mixed. There is an environment of 1,000 pupils from 11 to 18 years. My professors are quite strict but comprehensive. I have too much homework to do all the evenings.

My school is very big and mixed. There are ~~roughly~~ 1,000 pupils aged 11 to 18 years old. My teachers are quite strict but understanding. I have too much homework to do every evening.

3 Translate these passages into English.

1 Au collège ma matière préférée c'est le dessin car je suis créatif, mais je déteste le français. C'est une matière difficile et je ne m'entends pas avec mon prof. J'ai choisi d'étudier l'espagnol car je pense que c'est utile et assez facile.

_____

_____

_____

_____

2 Je n'aime pas mon collège. La journée scolaire est trop longue et le règlement est sévère. On ne peut pas porter de bijoux et selon moi c'est ridicule. Je vais passer des examens cet été, donc il faut faire beaucoup de travail scolaire.

_____

_____

_____

H **4** **Read this passage and complete the partial translation below.**

> If you don't know this, try to work it out from *blanc* and *interactif*. What could this be in a school classroom?

Mon collège est très bien équipé. Nous avons un tableau blanc interactif dans toutes les classes et il y a plein d'ordinateurs. Je suis ici depuis quatre ans et je trouve les profs travailleurs et gentils. Je suis fort en maths mais faible en langues, alors mon meilleur copain m'aide avec mes devoirs d'anglais.

> *Faible* looks like 'feeble' in English, so can you work out a better word for it here?

> Remember, this means 'for' in this case.

My school is very **1** _____ . We have an **2** _____ and there are lots of computers. I **3** _____ four years and I find the teachers **4** _____ . I am good at maths but **5** _____ , so **6** _____ my English homework.

H **5** **Translate these passages into English.**

1 J'adore mon collège et l'anglais m'intéresse particulièrement. Je viens de rentrer d'une visite scolaire en Angleterre et j'ai pu améliorer mon anglais en parlant aux ados là-bas. Nous avons passé une semaine à Bath où j'ai aimé voir les vieux bâtiments et l'église impressionnante au centre-ville. J'espère y retourner.

2 Quand j'étais plus jeune j'allais à une petite école primaire qui m'a beaucoup plu. Malheureusement mon lycée est trop grand à mon avis et le règlement est strict et complètement bête. Je ne comprends pas pourquoi je ne peux pas avoir un piercing et je voudrais pouvoir me teindre les cheveux.

3 En Angleterre les élèves doivent porter un uniforme scolaire, ce qui encourage la bonne discipline et cache les différences entre les riches et les pauvres. Dans mon collège on peut porter ce qu'on veut mais je n'aime pas ça parce qu'il y a ceux qui mettent des vêtements chers et chics pour montrer qu'ils ont beaucoup d'argent.

1a Read this passage and translate the French words below into English.

> Je vais bientôt quitter mon lycée. J'ai l'intention de continuer mes études de maths à l'université parce que dans le futur je voudrais trouver un emploi bien payé. Je pense que je vais aller à une université qui est située près de la maison de mes parents.

1 bientôt _____

2 continuer mes études _____

3 à l'avenir _____

4 trouver _____

5 bien payé _____

6 près de _____

> ⭐ Adverbs like *bientôt* come <u>after</u> the verb in French, but you will need to find the most natural place to put them in your translation into English.

b Now translate the whole passage into English.

_____

_____

_____

_____

2 Read this passage and complete the partial translation below. The missing words are all verbs.

> Je voudrais voyager à l'étranger parce que j'aimerais visiter des pays différents comme les États-Unis ou la Chine. Ma mère a déjà visité New York et l'a trouvé super. Mon rêve est d'acheter une voiture rapide, alors je (pourrais) aussi aller partout en France.

I would **1** *like to travel* abroad because I would **2** *like to visit* different countries like the USA or China. My mother **3** *has already visited* New York and **4** *she found* it great. My dream **5** *is to buy* a fast car, so I **6** *could also go* ~~to~~ everywhere in France too.

3 Translate these passages into English.

1 Plus tard dans la vie j'ai l'intention de me marier et je voudrais avoir deux ou trois enfants. Mon rêve est de devenir pilote car j'adore les avions. Je veux aussi faire un tour du monde avec ma famille. Surtout j'aimerais être heureux.

_____

_____

_____

_____

2 Je ne sais pas exactement ce que je vais faire dans la vie, mais je pense que je voudrais continuer à étudier le dessin parce qu'on dit que je suis artistique. Je ne veux pas me marier puisque mes parents ont divorcé il y a cinq ans.

_____

_____

_____

_____

🅗 4a The underlined verbs all express future intentions. Translate them into English.

Plus tard dans la vie **1** je voyagerai partout dans le monde puisque **2** je rêve de découvrir d'autres cultures étrangères. **3** J'espère aussi travailler ailleurs dans le futur. **4** Mon frère aimerait habiter en Australie car il aime le climat chaud là-bas. **5** Je compte aller à la fac et **6** j'ai l'intention d'être riche un jour.

1 _____   3 _____   5 _____

2 _____   4 _____   6 _____

🅗 b Now translate the whole passage into English.

> ⭐ Some of the verbs are followed by an infinitive in French. Take care when translating these into English.

_____
_____
_____
_____

🅗 5 Translate these passages into English.

1 Quand je quitterai l'école je compte aller à l'université étudier la physique. Après avoir fini mes études mon ambition est de devenir ingénieur comme mon père. Il dit que c'est un emploi intéressant et stimulant, donc il aime beaucoup son travail. J'espère travailler pour une entreprise où je pourrais utiliser mes compétences.

_____
_____
_____
_____

2 L'année prochaine je voudrais faire un apprentissage dans un garage parce que le travail technique me plaît énormément et être mécanicien m'a toujours attiré. Mon rêve est de construire ma propre voiture mais je sais que ce sera très difficile. Si je travaille dur je trouverai peut-être un emploi satisfaisant et assez bien payé et je serai heureux.

_____
_____
_____
_____

3 Plus tard dans la vie, j'aimerais faire du bénévolat en Afrique car je crois qu'il est important d'aider les gens défavorisés, surtout les pauvres. Mes parents m'ont toujours encouragé à penser aux autres, alors je voudrais essayer d'améliorer la vie de ceux qui n'ont pas grand-chose. Je m'intéresse aux sciences et dans le futur j'espère étudier la médecine.

_____
_____
_____
_____

Translation: English–French Strategies

There are some different strategies to consider when you are translating from English into French, partly because you will be able to understand the text you see so you don't need to try to work out any meanings before you start. However, most people would consider that translating into French is more difficult.

When you have a passage or sentence to translate into French, read the whole thing through once. Then work sentence by sentence or phrase by phrase bearing the following strategies in mind.

Grammar

Verbs

- Read the English carefully to make sure you have identified which <u>tense</u> needs to be used in French. Look for clues such as time markers to help you.

  Yesterday I went swimming. ➔ <u>perfect tense</u> needed

  Tomorrow I'm going to go shopping. ➔ <u>future tense</u> needed

  But remember that to say you <u>have been doing</u> something for a certain length of time in French, you use *depuis* + the present tense, when you would use the perfect tense in English. Don't let this catch you out!

  I have been learning Spanish for four years.   *Je parle espagnol depuis quatre ans.*

- Think carefully about the verb forms you need. Who is the subject of the verb (who is doing the action)? Is it more than one person? Make sure you know your verb endings. For the perfect tense, check you have used the correct auxiliary verb (*avoir* or *être*) and a past participle.

  She arrived late.   *Elle est arrivée en retard.*

  > Remember that with verbs using *être* in the perfect tense, the past participle must agree with the subject of the verb.

- Look out for <u>reflexive verbs</u> in French as these aren't always obvious from the English.

  I get up at 8 o'clock.   *Je me lève à 8 heures.*

- Remember that French uses <u>infinitives</u> when English uses words ending in '–ing'.

  I like **playing** squash.   *J'aime **jouer** au squash.*

- You might have to use <u>modal verbs</u>, so look out for 'can', 'must', should', 'allowed to' and remember that these verb forms are followed by the infinitive in French.

  You **can** do watersports.   *On **peut** faire des sports nautiques.*

- **H** Look out also for 'could', 'had to' and 'was allowed to', which will mean you need to use modal verbs in the <u>imperfect tense</u>.

- Look out for 'would' in the English. This will indicate that you need the <u>conditional</u> in French.

Nouns and adjectives

- Gender, articles and adjectival agreement and position are also really important when you are translating nouns into French.

  She has a **big** house.   *Elle a une **grande** maison.*

  He was wearing **black** gloves. *Il portait des gants **noirs**.*

  I saw two **grey** mice.   *J'ai vu deux souris **grises**.*

  > Remember that you must add an *–e* to most adjectives when they describe a feminine noun, *–s* when they describe a masculine plural noun and *–es* when they describe a feminine plural noun.

Time phrases

- Learn common time and frequency phrases so you always have them ready to use: yesterday (*hier*), today (*aujourd'hui*), tomorrow (*demain*), every day (*tous les jours*), etc.

Useful little words

- Build up your bank of vocabulary with useful little words, which you are likely to need in your translations, for example: <u>intensifiers</u> (quite – *assez*, very – *très*), <u>quantifiers</u> (a lot of – *beaucoup de*, a little – *un peu de*), <u>conjunctions</u> (but – *mais*), because – *parce que*), <u>prepositions</u> (on – *sur*, near – *près de*).

Studio GCSE French © Pearson Education Limited 2016

Word order

- You need to think carefully about word order when you are translating into French. Remember the rules for adjectives, object pronouns and, to a lesser extent, adverbs:

Adjectives

I bought some **black** shoes.   *J'ai acheté des chaussures **noires**.*

> Most adjectives, including all colours, come <u>after</u> the verb they describe.

Object pronouns

I saw **him** yesterday.   *Je **l'**ai vu hier.*

> The pronoun *l'* comes <u>before</u> the verb and, in the perfect tense, before the auxiliary verb.

Adverbs

I **also** like rugby.   *J'aime **aussi** le rugby.*

> Adverbs often come <u>after</u> the verb in French, even when they come elsewhere in the sentence in English.

Translation skills

- Be careful with words which we miss out in English but which must be there in French, and vice versa.

I watched TV yesterday.   *J'ai regardé **la** télé hier.*

> The word for 'the' must be used in French.

On Saturdays she does her homework.   *Le samedi elle fait ses devoirs.*

> No word for 'on' here in French.

I want to be **a** doctor.   *Je veux être docteur.*

> Remember that you don't use an article with jobs in French.

- Avoid translating word for word when you translate into French. It is often not possible to do this.
  Be particularly careful with the continuous present in English, which cannot be directly translated into French – remember, you just need the present tense in French.

I **am** studying French at university.   *J'étudie le français à l'université.*

> No word for 'am/is/are' with 'studying' in French.

Similarly, you cannot translate the imperfect tense in French word for word.

I **was** crossing the road / I **used to** cross the road.   *Je **traversais** la rue.*

> No separate word in French for 'was/were' or 'used to'.

The same is true for 'will' in the future tense and 'would' in the conditional: they are not separate words in French.

They **will arrive** at 6 o'clock.   *Ils **arriveront** à six heures.*
I **would prefer** to play football.   *Je **préférerais** jouer au foot.*

- We are sometimes a little lazy with our written English, but French does not allow this.

The man I know…   *L'homme **que** je connais…*

> In English a more correct way to say this would be 'the man whom I know', and *que* is needed here in French. So bear this in mind when translating into French.

- When you are asked to translate from English into French, you might need to look carefully at the sentence or part of the sentence which comes <u>before</u> the one you are translating.

The house which we bought is too small.

La maison *que nous avons acheté**e** est trop petit**e**.*

> *La maison* is at the start of the sentence but because it is feminine, you need to add an extra *e* on the past participle *acheté**e*** and the adjective *petit**e***.

- If you don't know how to say something in French, don't panic! Try to think of a synonym, a similar word, or another way to say it using vocabulary that you <u>do</u> know.
- Check your spelling, accents and grammar!
- If you have time, it is a good idea to try to translate what you have written back into English, to see if it really does match the translation you were asked to do.

As you are working through the translations on the following pages, try to avoid using translation software, lots of which is available online. Although online dictionaries can be helpful for individual nouns, there is no guarantee that any online translation service can provide you with a correct answer in any context. Don't just accept the first answer you find!

Look at this sentence in English and its French translation. Try to see how the translation was made.

> My favourite hobby is roller-blading because it is exciting.
> *Mon passe-temps préféré est le roller parce que c'est passionnant.*

Note that because 'favourite' is an adjective, it comes <u>after</u> the word it describes in French, even though it comes <u>before</u> the noun in English. Note also that 'it is' and 'it's' are the same thing, but both would be translated here by the French *c'est*.

Now look at this sentence:

> I prefer windsurfing because I like water sports.

This sentence asks you for 'I prefer' in the present tense, which is easier since it does not need to agree. 'Windsurfing' is a noun so it will need the correct definite article (*le* or *la*) in French to show its gender. 'I like' should be easy since you use this word all the time. However, with 'water sports' you will need the word for 'the' to show that it is plural and you will also need to change the word order to 'sports' + adjective (*nautique*), which will need to <u>agree</u> with the noun (*sports*).

So, the translation will be:

> *Je préfère la planche à voile parce que j'aime les sports nautiques.*

1 **Complete the translations of these sentences. The first four have been partially translated to help you.**

1 I go to the cinema with my friends.

  Je vais au cinéma *avec mes amis*

2 He likes documentaries because they are interesting.

  Il aime les documentaires *parce qu'ils sont intéressant*

3 My sister is lazy and chatty.

  Ma sœur *est paraseuse et bavarde.*

4 Every Saturday I go shopping in town.

  Tous les samedis *je vais faire du shopping en ville.*

5 In my family there are five people.

6 You can go swimming at the sports centre.

7 He doesn't get on well with his parents.

8 Cathy played football yesterday but unfortunately her team lost.

9 I would like to go windsurfing because it's fun.

10 I listened to music on my mobile because it's easy.

H 2 **Read this passage and complete the partial translation below.**

> Think about word order in this sentence as there is a direct object pronoun.

Texts are quicker and easier than a phone call, but I never use social media sites because you can reveal too many personal details. I think it's dangerous. My sister often uses them and she has made a lot of new friends, but she spends hours on line and I would prefer to do other things.

> The word 'that' hasn't been used here in English, but the French word for it needs to be included in your translation.

Les textos sont plus **1** .... qu'un appel mais

2 .... les réseaux sociaux car on peut révéler trop de détails personnels.

Je **3** .... Ma sœur **4** .... et elle

s'est fait beaucoup de nouveaux amis, mais **5** .... et

je **6** .... autre chose.

H 3 **Translate these passages into French.**

1   When I was younger I used to play tennis in summer and go mountain biking in winter, but now I prefer to go rock climbing. It's an interesting hobby but my parents think that it's too dangerous, especially when it's raining. In the future I would like to try archery because it's different.

....

....

....

....

....

2   A good friend is someone who listens to your problems and is always there for you. I have known my best friend, Lucien, for eleven years and we do a lot of things together. Last week we went to a football match and our team won. Tomorrow he is playing the guitar in a rock music concert.

....

....

....

....

....

Look at this sentence, which needs to be translated.

> I like going on holiday to Spain.

You will probably know *J'aime*, *vacances* and *Espagne*, but the words 'going' and 'to' might cause problems. Here, 'going' in French would need to be an infinitive after *J'aime* – remember that in English we might also say 'I like to go'. The word for 'to' with a feminine country (most countries are feminine in French) is *en*, so the translation of the sentence would be:

> *J'aime aller en vacances en Espagne.*

Now look at this sentence.

> She lives in a small town.

In this sentence, the grammar is quite simple – you just need one verb in the present tense. However, notice that the subject of the sentence here is 'she', so you need to make sure you use the third person he/she ending of the verb here. You also need a different word for 'in' – when you talk about countries, etc. you use 'en', but for other locations you need 'dans'.

You need to think about the vocabulary as well. You will need to remember that *petit* (small) is one of the few adjectives which come <u>before</u> the noun being described. You must also remember that *la ville* (town) is a feminine noun, so the adjective needs to agree with the noun.

The correct translation is:

> *Elle habite dans une petite ville.*

1 Translate these sentences into French. The first four have been partially translated to help you.

1 He prefers travelling by car.

Il préfère .

2 Usually I spend my holidays in France.

D'habitude je passe .

3 In my village there isn't a cinema.

Dans mon village .

4 My friends often go skiing in Switzerland.

Mes amis font .

5 In my town you can visit an historic castle.

6 There are lots of tourists in summer.

7 We normally travel to Portugal by plane.

8 Last year I went to New York to celebrate my birthday.

9 I would like to visit Australia because it's hot there.

10 There is nothing for young people in my region, so it's boring.

H 2 **Look at this passage in English and complete the partial translation below.**

> In my region there are lots of things to do. You can go to the theatre or the new ice rink and there is a museum and an old church for those who are interested in history. Yesterday I went to the sports centre with my best friend and we played badminton. In summer there is a music festival.

Dans ma région **1** _____. On peut

2 _____ et il y a un musée et

3 _____ pour **4** _____l'histoire.

Hier **5** _____ avec mon meilleur copain et

6 _____. En été **7**_____ .

H 3 **Read the English text and correct the French translation below. The mistakes have been crossed out.**

> My favourite means of transport is the plane because it is so fast. I know that there are sometimes problems at the airport but I listen to some music to pass the time. I don't like travelling by car because there is too much traffic. My brother likes travelling by train but I find that tiring.

Mon **1** ~~préféré moyen de transport~~ _____ est l'avion **2** ~~parce qu'~~ _____ c'est **3** ~~donc~~ _____ rapide. Je sais qu'il y a quelquefois des problèmes à l'aéroport mais **4** ~~j'ai écouté~~ _____ de la musique pour passer le temps. Je n'aime pas **5** ~~voyageant~~ _____ en **6** ~~car~~ _____ parce qu'il y a **7** ~~trop circulation~~ _____ . **8** ~~Ma frère~~ _____ aime voyager en train mais je **9** ~~trouvé~~ _____ ça **10** ~~fatigué~~ _____ .

H 4 **Translate these passages into French.**

1 I usually go on holiday with my family but last year I went camping with some friends in Scotland. We travelled by train and the journey was very pleasant. Unfortunately it rained from time to time but we went to the swimming pool and the cinema. Next year I will go to Italy to spend a few days with my uncle.

_____

_____

_____

_____

_____

2 In the future I would like to visit America. I have never been there but they say that the people are nice. My mother doesn't like going abroad because she prefers English cooking. We went to Morocco two years ago and she hated the spicy food in the restaurant at our hotel.

_____

_____

_____

_____

1 **Translate these sentences into French. The sentences have been started and there are tips to help you.**

> 'Save' might be 'economise' in English.

> 'Energy' will need an article because it is a noun.

1   We must save energy.

On doit _economiser l'énergie_ .

> The verb will be plural.

> 'Pollution' will need an article.

2   Factories cause pollution.

Les usines _de provoquer des pollutions_

2 **Translate these sentences into French. The first four have been partially translated to help you.**

1   Our planet is in danger.

Notre planète _en danger_ .

2   Pollution is a serious problem.

La pollution est _un problème grave_ .

3   I like to help animals.

J'aime _aider des animaux_ .

4   Our climate is warmer now.

Notre climat _est plus chaud maintenant_ .

5   I think that fair trade is important.

Je pense que le commerce équitable

6   There is a big music festival in Montreux.

Il y a un festival de musique grand à Montreux

7   I would like to eat more healthily.

8   It is important to protect the forests to help wild animals.

9   Tomorrow I am going to start an online campaign against poverty.

10   Hunger is a big problem in Africa and governments should do more.

H 3 Read this English passage and complete the partial translation below with the correct verbs.

> To save the Earth we can all do something to help. I try to go to school on foot or by bike if possible. My family has reduced its consumption of gas and electricity and my mum has stopped going to work by car. If we can reduce pollution, we will safeguard the world.

Afin de **1** _____ la Terre **2** _____ tous faire quelque chose pour aider.

3 _____ au collège à pied ou en vélo si possible. Ma famille

4 _____ sa consommation de gaz et d'électricité et ma mère

5 _____ au travail en voiture. Si nous **6** _____ la

pollution nous **7** _____ le monde.

💡 Take great care with tenses when you are translating. There is a mix of many different ones for you to deal with here.

H 4 Translate these passages into French.

1 Many small islands are threatened by the level of the sea which is going to increase every year because of global warming. There are more earthquakes and floods too. If we do not help the poorest countries of the world, there will be more drought and famine and people will suffer.

_____

_____

_____

_____

_____

_____

2 Events like the World Cup can help us to discover different cultures and countries. I think that it's important to understand how people live elsewhere in the world and when I went to a rugby festival in Canada I learned to respect others and made lots of new friends.

_____

_____

_____

_____

_____

_____

💡 Remember that you may need to re-phrase or find a slightly different word to translate successfully.

1a Complete the translation of this sentence.

Lessons start at half past eight.

Remember that you will need to start with 'the lessons', as in French you can't just have the word 'lessons' alone.

commencement
les cours commencent à huit heures et demie.

Don't forget to make the verb plural.

b Correct this translation.

There is a football club after school.

Il y a un ~~foot club~~ après collège.
club de foot

Remember that there will be an extra word somewhere in the French, and that word order might be an issue here.

2 Translate these sentences into French. The first four have been partially translated to help you.

1 My favourite subject is drama.

Mon cour préféré est l'art dramatique.

2 I like French because it's useful.

J'aime le français parce que c'est utile.

3 You cannot wear trainers at my school.

On ne peut pas porter des baskets dans mon collège.

4 The teachers are funny and intelligent.

Les professeurs sont drôle et intelligentes.

5 There is a break which lasts 20 minutes.

Il y a un recreation qui.

6 I am good at maths.

7 Last year I went on a school trip to the museum.

8 I am going to go on a school exchange next summer and I hope to visit Paris.

9 I get a lot of homework in science and I hate that.

10 My English teacher gets on my nerves because he is strict.

Studio GCSE French © Pearson Education Limited 2016

H 3 Read this passage about school and complete the partial translation below with the correct word or phrase.

> My school day begins too early in my opinion. I go to school by bus and yesterday I arrived late. There are four lessons in the morning and we have a break at 11:00. There is only one lesson in the afternoon and we finish at 3:15. Last week I stayed at school until 6:00. I played football for my school team. Next week I'm going to play basketball after school.

Ma journée scolaire **1** _____ trop tôt à mon avis. Je **2** _____ au collège en bus et hier je **3** _____ en retard. **4** _____ quatre cours le matin et nous **5** _____ une récréation à onze heures. **6** _____ seulement un cours l'après-midi et nous **7** _____ à quinze heures quinze. La semaine dernière **8** _____ au collège jusqu'à six heures. J'**9**_____ au foot pour l'équipe de mon collège. La semaine prochaine je **10** _____ au basket après le collège.

> You will need to make sure that you use the correct tense here. The first 7 verbs are in the present tense, **8** and **9** need the perfect tense and **10** needs the near future tense. Be careful – one of the perfect tenses is a verb which uses *être* as auxiliary!

H 4 Translate these passages into French.

1   When I was younger I used to like PE but now it's boring. I have chosen to study history because I get on well with my teacher. I get good marks in music but I'm weak at geography. I find the school rules fair but I would prefer to be able to wear jewellery.

_____

_____

_____

_____

2   There are about one thousand pupils in my school. The buildings are very modern but there is no swimming pool and the canteen is too small. There are lots of clubs after school and you can do a range of sports like athletics and volleyball. Last month I went on a school exchange to Spain.

_____

_____

_____

_____

_____

1a Translate this sentence into French.

I want to work in a bank. ....

> Which gender is bank?

- Try splitting the sentence into three parts as this can help you focus more closely:
  I want / to work / in a bank.
- Think about which irregular verb you need for 'I want' and decide on the correct form.
- What part of the verb is 'to work'?

b Now translate this sentence into French.

> Try and use one set expression for each of these phrases.

Next year I would like to find a job.

....

2 Translate these sentences into French. The first four have been partially translated to help you.

1 I would like to get married.

Je voudrais ....

2 My friend works in a supermarket.

.... dans un supermarché .

3 I don't want to work in an office.

.... travailler dans ....

4 I would like to be a dentist.

Je voudrais ....

5 Next year I am going to study biology.

....

6 I intend to go to Canada.

....

7 My brother is going to go to university in September.

....

8 In the future my ambition is to visit my aunt in Australia.

....

9 I hope to get married and have a son and a daughter as I like children.

....

10 I work in a clothes shop with my friends at the weekend.

....

H **3** **Translate this passage into French. The first sentence has been broken down for you in the strategy box.**

> I would like to do an apprenticeship after having left school as I think it will be interesting and useful. I hope to be an engineer but I know that the training is quite long and difficult. My uncle works as an engineer in a factory where they make engines for aeroplanes.

Look at each sentence and try to break it down into manageable parts:

I would like / to do an apprenticeship / after having left school / as I think / (that) it will be interesting and useful.

Je voudrais / faire un apprentissage / après avoir quitté le collège / comme je pense / qu'il sera intéressant et utile.

Do the same for the other two sentences, taking care with articles for jobs, adjectives which need to agree and the need for articles before French words where they don't exist in English.

....

....

....

....

....

H **4** **Translate these passages into French.**

1 When I'm older I would like to travel because I think that it's really important to discover other cultures and to meet people from different areas. If I had lots of money my dream would be to spend some time in China or Japan as I'd like to visit different countries.

....

....

....

....

....

2 After leaving university I plan to do some voluntary work abroad. I have decided that I would like to become a doctor because it is a profession where you can help people. There will be difficult exams but if I pass I'll find a job in a hospital.

....

....

....

....

....

Regular verbs

Learn the patterns for –er, –ir and –re verbs and you can use any regular verbs!

INFINITIVE	PRESENT TENSE (stem + present tense endings)	PERFECT TENSE (auxiliary + past participle)	IMPERFECT TENSE (stem + imperfect endings)	FUTURE TENSE (infinitive + future endings)	CONDITIONAL (infinitive + conditional endings)
regarder to watch	je regard<u>e</u> tu regardes il regarde nous regardons vous regardez ils regardent	j'ai regardé tu as regardé il a regardé nous avons regardé vous avez regardé ils ont regardé	je regardais tu regardais il regardait nous regardions vous regardiez ils regardaient	je regarderai tu regarderas il regardera nous regarderons vous regarderez ils regarderont	je regarderais tu regarderais il regarderait nous regarderions vous regarderiez ils regarderaient
finir to finish	je finis tu finis il finit nous finissons vous finissez ils finissent	j'ai fini tu as fini il a fini nous avons fini vous avez fini ils ont fini	je finissais tu finissais il finissait nous finissions vous finissiez ils finissaient	je finirai tu finiras il finira nous finirons vous finirez ils finiront	je finirais tu finirais il finirait nous finirions vous finiriez ils finiraient
attendre to wait	j'attends tu attends il attend nous attendons vous attendez ils attendent	j'ai attendu tu as attendu il a attendu nous avons attendu vous avez attendu ils ont attendu	j'attendais tu attendais il attendait nous attendions vous attendiez ils attendaient	j'attendrai tu attendras il attendra nous attendrons vous attendrez ils attendront	j'attendrais tu attendrais il attendrait nous attendrions vous attendriez ils attendraient
se connecter to connect	je me connecte tu te connectes il se connecte nous nous connectons vous vous connectez ils se connectent	je me suis connecté(e) tu t'es connecté(e) il s'est connecté nous nous sommes connecté(e)s vous vous êtes connecté(e)(s) ils se sont connectés	je me connectais tu te connectais il se connectait nous nous connections vous vous connectiez ils se connectaient	je me connecterai tu te connecteras il se connectera nous nous connecterons vous vous connecterez ils se connecteront	je me connecterais tu te connecterais il se connecterait nous nous connecterions vous vous connecteriez ils se connecteraient

Here is a list of useful regular –er, –ir and –re verbs that you can learn:

Regular –er verbs:

aimer	to love	habiter	to live	remarquer	to notice
arriver	to arrive	inviter	to invite	retrouver	to find
bavarder	to chat	jouer	to play	télécharger	to download
chanter	to sing	louer	to rent	tomber	to fall
chercher	to look for	parler	to talk	tourner	to turn
continuer	to continue	penser	to think	travailler	to work
décider	to decide	porter	to wear	trouver	to find
écouter	to listen	préparer	to prepare	visiter	to visit
fumer	to smoke	profiter	to make the most of	voyager	to travel
gagner	to win	regarder	to look		

Regular –ir verbs:

choisir	to choose	rougir	to blush	réussir	to succeed

Regular –re verbs:

attendre	to wait	perdre	to lose	répondre	to reply
vendre	to sell				

Studio GCSE French © Pearson Education Limited 2016

Key irregular verbs

INFINITIVE	PRESENT TENSE (watch out for the change of stems)	PERFECT TENSE (auxiliary + past participle)	IMPERFECT TENSE (stem + imperfect endings)	FUTURE TENSE (stem + future endings)	CONDITIONAL (stem + conditional endings)
avoir to have	j'**ai** tu **as** il **a** nous **avons** vous **avez** ils **ont**	j'ai **eu** tu as eu il a eu nous avons eu vous avez eu ils ont eu	j'avais tu avais il avait nous avions vous aviez ils avaient	j'**aur**ai tu auras il aura nous aurons vous aurez ils auront	j'**aur**ais tu aurais il aurait nous aurions vous auriez ils auraient
être to be	je **suis** tu **es** il **est** nous **sommes** vous **êtes** ils **sont**	j'ai **été** tu as été il a été nous avons été vous avez été ils ont été	j'**étais** tu étais il était nous étions vous étiez ils étaient	je **ser**ai tu seras il sera nous serons vous serez ils seront	je **ser**ais tu serais il serait nous serions vous seriez ils seraient
faire to do, make	je **fais** tu **fais** il **fait** nous **faisons** vous **faites** ils **font**	j'ai **fait** tu as fait il a fait nous avons fait vous avez fait ils ont fait	je faisais tu faisais il faisait nous faisions vous faisiez ils faisaient	je **fer**ai tu feras il fera nous ferons vous ferez ils feront	je **fer**ais tu ferais il ferait nous ferions vous feriez ils feraient
aller to go	je **vais** tu **vas** il **va** nous allons vous allez ils **vont**	je **suis** allé(e) tu **es** allé(e) il **est** allé nous **sommes** allé(e)s vous **êtes** allé(e)(s) ils **sont** allés	j'allais tu allais il allait nous allions vous alliez ils allaient	j'**ir**ai tu iras il ira nous irons vous irez ils iront	j'**ir**ais tu irais il irait nous irions vous iriez ils iraient
prendre to take (*also applies to* apprendre, comprendre)	je **prends** tu **prends** il **prend** nous **prenons** vous **prenez** ils **prennent**	j'ai **pris** tu as pris il a pris nous avons pris vous avez pris ils ont pris	je prenais tu prenais il prenait nous prenions vous preniez ils prenaient	je prendrai tu prendras il prendra nous prendrons vous prendrez ils prendront	je prendrais tu prendrais il prendrait nous prendrions vous prendriez ils prendraient

The following key irregular verbs are known as 'modal' verbs.

INFINITIVE	PRESENT TENSE (watch out for the change of stems)	PERFECT TENSE (auxiliary + past participle)	IMPERFECT TENSE (stem + imperfect endings)	FUTURE TENSE (stem + future endings)	CONDITIONAL (stem + conditional endings)
vouloir to want	je **veux** tu **veux** il **veut** nous **voulons** vous **voulez** ils **veulent**	j'ai **voulu** tu as voulu il a voulu nous avons voulu vous avez voulu ils ont voulu	je voulais tu voulais il voulait nous voulions vous vouliez ils voulaient	je **voudr**ai tu voudras il voudra nous voudrons vous voudrez ils voudront	je **voudr**ais tu voudrais il voudrait nous voudrions vous voudriez ils voudraient
pouvoir can / to be able to	je **peux** tu **peux** il **peut** nous **pouvons** vous **pouvez** ils **peuvent**	j'ai **pu** tu as pu il a pu nous avons pu vous avez pu ils ont pu	je pouvais tu pouvais il pouvait nous pouvions vous pouviez ils pouvaient	je **pourr**ai tu pourras il pourra nous pourrons vous pourrez ils pourront	je **pourr**ais tu pourrais il pourrait nous pourrions vous pourriez ils pourraient
devoir must / to have to	je **dois** tu **dois** il **doit** nous **devons** vous **devez** ils **doivent**	j'ai **dû** tu as dû il a dû nous avons dû vous avez dû ils ont dû	je devais tu devais il devait nous devions vous deviez ils devaient	je **devr**ai tu devras il devra nous devrons vous devrez ils devront	je **devr**ais tu devrais il devrait nous devrions vous devriez ils devraient

Verb tables

Other useful irregular verbs

INFINITIVE	PRESENT TENSE (watch out for the change of stems)	PERFECT TENSE (auxiliary + past participle)	IMPERFECT TENSE (stem + imperfect endings)	FUTURE TENSE (stem + future endings)	CONDITIONAL (stem + conditional endings)
boire to drink	je **bois** tu bois il boit nous **buv**ons vous **buv**ez ils **boiv**ent	j'ai **bu** tu as bu il a bu nous avons bu vous avez bu ils ont bu	je buvais tu buvais il buvait nous buvions vous buviez ils buvaient	je boirai tu boiras il boira nous boirons vous boirez ils boiront	je boirais tu boirais il boirait nous boirions vous boiriez ils boiraient
conduire to drive	je **condui**s tu conduis il conduit nous **conduis**ons vous conduisez ils conduisent	j'ai **conduit** tu as conduit il a conduit nous avons conduit vous avez conduit ils ont conduit	je conduisais tu conduisais il conduisait nous conduisions vous conduisiez ils conduisaient	je conduirai tu conduiras il conduira nous conduirons vous conduirez ils conduiront	je conduirais tu conduirais il conduirait nous conduirions vous conduiriez ils conduiraient
connaître to know	je **connai**s tu connais il connaît nous **connaiss**ons vous connaissez ils connaissent	j'ai **connu** tu as connu il a connu nous avons connu vous avez connu ils ont connu	je connaissais tu connaissais il connaissait nous connaissions vous connaissiez ils connaissaient	je connaîtrai tu connaîtras il connaîtra nous connaîtrons vous connaîtrez ils connaîtront	je connaîtrais tu connaîtrais il connaîtrait nous connaîtrions vous connaîtriez ils connaîtraient
croire to believe	je **crois** tu crois il croit nous **croy**ons vous croyez ils **croi**ent	j'ai **cru** tu as cru il a cru nous avons cru vous avez cru ils ont cru	je croyais tu croyais il croyait nous croyions vous croyiez ils croyaient	je croirai tu croiras il croira nous croirons vous croirez ils croiront	je croirais tu croirais il croirait nous croirions vous croiriez ils croiraient
dire to say	je **dis** tu dis il dit nous **dis**ons vous dites ils disent	j'ai **dit** tu as dit il a dit nous avons dit vous avez dit ils ont dit	je disais tu disais il disait nous disions vous disiez ils disaient	je dirai tu diras il dira nous dirons vous direz ils diront	je dirais tu dirais il dirait nous dirions vous diriez ils diraient
dormir to sleep	je **dor**s tu dors il dort nous **dorm**ons vous dormez ils dorment	j'ai dormi tu as dormi il a dormi nous avons dormi vous avez dormi ils ont dormi	je dormais tu dormais il dormait nous dormions vous dormiez ils dormaient	je dormirai tu dormiras il dormira nous dormirons vous dormirez ils dormiront	je dormirais tu dormirais il dormirait nous dormirions vous dormiriez ils dormiraient
écrire to write	j'**écris** tu écris il écrit nous **écriv**ons vous écrivez ils écrivent	j'ai **écrit** tu as écrit il a écrit nous avons écrit vous avez écrit ils ont écrit	j'écrivais tu écrivais il écrivait nous écrivions vous écriviez ils écrivaient	j'écrirai tu écriras il écrira nous écrirons vous écrirez ils écriront	j'écrirais tu écrirais il écrirait nous écririons vous écririez ils écriraient
envoyer to send	j'**envoi**e tu envoies il envoie nous **envoy**ons vous envoyez ils **envoi**ent	j'ai envoyé tu as envoyé il a envoyé nous avons envoyé vous avez envoyé ils ont envoyé	j'envoyais tu envoyais il envoyait nous envoyions vous envoyiez ils envoyaient	j'**enverr**ai tu enverras il enverra nous enverrons vous enverrez ils enverront	j'**enverr**ais tu enverrais il enverrait nous enverrions vous enverriez ils enverraient
essayer to try	j'**essai**e tu essaies il essaie nous **essay**ons vous essayez ils **essai**ent	j'ai essayé tu as essayé il a essayé nous avons essayé vous avez essayé ils ont essayé	j'essayais tu essayais il essayait nous essayions vous essayiez ils essayaient	j'**essaier**ai tu essaieras il essaiera nous essaierons vous essaierez ils essaieront	j'**essaier**ais tu essaierais il essaierait nous essaierions vous essaieriez ils essaieraient
lire to read	je **lis** tu lis il lit nous **lis**ons vous lisez ils lisent	j'ai **lu** tu as lu il a lu nous avons lu vous avez lu ils ont lu	je lisais tu lisais il lisait nous lisions vous lisiez ils lisaient	je lirai tu liras il lira nous lirons vous lirez ils liront	je lirais tu lirais il lirait nous lirions vous liriez ils liraient

Studio GCSE French © Pearson Education Limited 2016

INFINITIVE	PRESENT TENSE (watch out for the change of stems)	PERFECT TENSE (auxiliary + past participle)	IMPERFECT TENSE (stem + imperfect endings)	FUTURE TENSE (stem + future endings)	CONDITIONAL (stem + conditional endings)
mettre to put	je **met**s tu mets il met nous **mett**ons vous mettez ils mettent	j'ai **mis** tu as mis il a mis nous avons mis vous avez mis ils ont mis	je mettais tu mettais il mettait nous mettions vous mettiez ils mettaient	je mettrai tu mettras il mettra nous mettrons vous mettrez ils mettront	je mettrais tu mettrais il mettrait nous mettrions vous mettriez ils mettraient
ouvrir to open	j'ouvr**e** tu ouvr**es** il ouvr**e** nous ouvr**ons** vous ouvr**ez** ils ouvr**ent**	j'ai **ouvert** tu as ouvert il a ouvert nous avons ouvert vous avez ouvert ils ont ouvert	j'ouvrais tu ouvrais il ouvrait nous ouvrions vous ouvriez ils ouvraient	j'ouvrirai tu ouvriras il ouvrira nous ouvrirons vous ouvrirez ils ouvriront	j'ouvrirais tu ouvrirais il ouvrirait nous ouvririons vous ouvririez ils ouvriraient
partir to leave	je **par**s tu pars il part nous **part**ons vous partez ils partent	je suis parti(e) tu es parti(e) il est parti nous sommes parti(e)s vous êtes parti(e)(s) ils sont partis	je partais tu partais il partait nous partions vous partiez ils partaient	je partirai tu partiras il partira nous partirons vous partirez ils partiront	je partirais tu partirais il partirait nous partirions vous partiriez ils partiraient
rire to laugh	je **ri**s tu ris il rit nous rions vous riez ils rient	j'ai ri tu as ri il a ri nous avons ri vous avez ri ils ont ri	je riais tu riais il riait nous riions vous riiez ils riaient	je rirai tu riras il rira nous rirons vous rirez ils riront	je rirais tu rirais il rirait nous ririons vous ririez ils riraient
savoir to know	je **sai**s tu sais il sait nous **sav**ons vous savez ils savent	j'ai **su** tu as su il a su nous avons su vous avez su ils ont su	je savais tu savais il savait nous savions vous saviez ils savaient	je **saur**ai tu sauras il saura nous saurons vous saurez ils sauront	je **saur**ais tu saurais il saurait nous saurions vous sauriez ils sauraient
se sentir to feel	je me **sen**s tu te sens il se sent nous nous **sent**ons vous vous sentez ils se sentent	je me suis senti(e) tu t'es senti(e) il s'est senti nous nous sommes senti(e)s vous vous êtes senti(e)(s) ils se sont sentis	je me sentais tu te sentais il se sentait nous nous sentions vous vous sentiez ils se sentaient	je me sentirai tu te sentiras il se sentira nous nous sentirons vous vous sentirez ils se sentiront	je me sentirais tu te sentirais il se sentirait nous nous sentirions vous vous sentiriez ils se sentiraient
sortir to go out, leave	je **sor**s tu sors il sort nous **sort**ons vous sortez ils sortent	je suis sorti(e) tu es sorti(e) il est sorti nous sommes sorti(e)s vous êtes sorti(e)(s) ils sont sortis	je sortais tu sortais il sortait nous sortions vous sortiez ils sortaient	je sortirai tu sortiras il sortira nous sortirons vous sortirez ils sortiront	je sortirais tu sortirais il sortirait nous sortirions vous sortiriez ils sortiraient
venir (*also applies to* devenir)	je **vien**s tu viens il vient nous **ven**ons vous venez ils **vienn**ent	je suis **venu**(e) tu es venu(e) il est venu nous sommes venu(e)s vous êtes venu(e)(s) ils sont venus	je venais tu venais il venait nous venions vous veniez ils venaient	je **viendr**ai tu viendras il viendra nous viendrons vous viendrez ils viendront	je **viendr**ais tu viendrais il viendrait nous viendrions vous viendriez ils viendraient
voir to see	je **voi**s tu vois il voit nous **voy**ons vous voyez ils **voi**ent	j'ai **vu** tu as vu il a vu nous avons vu vous avez vu ils ont vu	je voyais tu voyais il voyait nous voyions vous voyiez ils voyaient	je **verr**ai tu verras il verra nous verrons vous verrez ils verront	je **verr**ais tu verrais il verrait nous verrions vous verriez ils verraient

Verb tables

Verbs ending in *–ger*, like *manger*, add an *e* in the *nous* form to make the *g* a soft sound.

INFINITIVE	PRESENT TENSE	PERFECT TENSE (auxiliary + past participle)	IMPERFECT TENSE (stem + imperfect endings)	FUTURE TENSE (stem + future endings)	CONDITIONAL (stem + conditional endings)
manger to eat (*also applies to* nager, partager, etc.)	je mange tu manges il mange nous mangeons vous mangez ils mangent	j'ai mangé tu as mangé il a mangé nous avons mangé vous avez mangé ils ont mangé	je mangeais tu mangeais il mangeait nous mangions vous mangiez ils mangeaient	je mangerai tu mangeras il mangera nous mangerons vous mangerez ils mangeront	je mangerais tu mangerais il mangerait nous mangerions vous mangeriez ils mangeraient

These verbs have a spelling change in the *je, tu, il* and *ils* forms that affects the pronunciation. They otherwise behave as regular *–er* verbs.

INFINITIVE	PRESENT TENSE (watch out for the change of stems)	PERFECT TENSE (auxiliary + past participle)	IMPERFECT TENSE (stem + imperfect endings)	FUTURE TENSE (stem + future endings)	CONDITIONAL (stem + conditional endings)
appeler to call	j'appelle tu appelles il appelle nous appelons vous appelez ils appellent	j'ai appelé tu as appelé il a appelé nous avons appelé vous avez appelé ils ont appelé	j'appelais j'appelais il appelait nous appelions vous appeliez ils appelaient	j'appellerai tu appelleras il appellera nous appellerons vous appellerez ils appelleront	j'appellerais tu appellerais il appellerait nous appellerions vous appelleriez ils appelleraient
jeter to throw	je jette tu jettes il jette nous jetons vous jetez ils jettent	j'ai jeté tu as jeté il a jeté nous avons jeté vous avez jeté ils ont jeté	je jetais tu jetais il jetait nous jetions vous jetiez ils jetaient	je jetterai tu jetteras il jettera nous jetterons vous jetterez ils jetteront	je jetterais tu jetterais il jetterait nous jetterions vous jetteriez ils jetteraient
se lever to get up	je me lève tu te lèves il se lève nous nous levons vous vous **levez** ils se lèvent	je me suis levé(e) tu t'es levé(e) il s'est levé nous nous sommes levé(e)s vous vous êtes levé(e)(s) ils se sont levés	je me levais tu te levais il se levait nous nous levions vous vous leviez ils se levaient	je me lèverai tu te lèveras il se lèvera nous nous lèverons vous vous lèverez ils se lèveront	je me lèverais tu te lèverais il se lèverait nous nous lèverions vous vous lèveriez ils se lèveraient
acheter to buy	j'achète tu achètes il achète nous achetons vous achetez ils achètent	j'ai acheté tu as acheté il a acheté nous avons acheté vous avez acheté ils ont acheté	j'achetais tu achetais il achetait nous achetions vous achetiez ils achetaient	j'achèterai tu achèteras il achètera nous achèterons vous achèterez ils achèteront	j'achèterais tu achèterais il achèterait nous achèterions vous achèteriez ils achèteraient
préférer to prefer	je préfère tu préfères il préfère nous préférons vous préférez ils préfèrent	j'ai préféré tu as préféré il a préféré nous avons préféré vous avez préféré ils ont préféré	je préférais tu préférais il préférait nous préférions vous préfériez ils préféraient	je préférerai tu préféreras il préférera nous préférerons vous préférerez ils préféreront	je préférerais tu préférerais il préférerait nous préférerions vous préféreriez ils préféreraient

Studio GCSE French © Pearson Education Limited 2016